To Carvoy 13.11 with Love, Carl 9/15/0

M000310829

WHEN I BECAME A PSYCHIATRIST, PEOPLE STOPPED WAVING ON MAIN STREET

A Medical Conversation

By
Carl S. Burak, MD, JD

Co-Author of
The Cradle Will Fall

STANTON & SAMUEL PUBLISHING
FLORIDA

This is a work of "faction." Everything in this book represents actual experience and conversation that I've had with many, many patients. The fictional Bradys represent all of these patients; so in a sense I know Lisa and Ben very well.

© 2006 by Stanton & Samuel LLC
All rights reserved.
Stanton & Samuel Publishing
482 Jacksonville Drive
Jacksonville Beach, Florida 32250

Printed in the United States of America

Library of Congress Cataloging in publication data:
Burak, Carl S.
   When I Became A Psychiatrist People Stopped Waving On Main Street:
   Information about mental health; the misunderstanding of psychiatry.
   2nd edition
   Library of Congress Control Number: 2006930688
   p. cm. ISBN 0-9723357-1-4

Notice: This book is not intended to alter treatment that may have been prescribed by your doctor. It is intended as an information volume only, not as a medical manual. It is our hope that the information provided will help you make informed decisions about your health.

Mention of specific medications in this book does not imply endorsement by the author or publisher. The names of medications used by Lisa or her family have been changed in order to avoid the appearance of endorsement.

Cover photographs © Diane Drysdale; 2005, Atlantic Beach, FL
Back cover photograph © Eli Burak; 2005, Windsor, VT

For my Parents,
Belle and Sam,
May they rest in peace.

For my special second Mom,
Shirley Shils
For all she does.

For my patients,
Who have taught me so much.

And most of all for my Wife,
Ronnie,
And my Son,
Eli,
For their love and support.

SPECIAL DEDICATION

To Edward Shils (1915-2004)

Edward Shils, my father-in-law, passed away in November 2004, six months shy of his ninetieth birthday. He worked full-time until the day he died. As one of many who eulogized him, I said, "I view Ed's life as a true epic, rich, creative and filled with passion and love."

I was twice blessed. I had a wonderful father who sadly passed away when I was twenty-six, about a year after Ronnie and I were married; so for thirty-six years Ed was a great "second father."

My first meeting with my future father-in-law came one June evening in 1967. I was beginning my final year of medical school and Ronnie (who I had met earlier that spring in Boston) was enjoying the summer in Philadelphia before her final year of college.

I had already met Ronnie's mother, Shirley, but Ed had never been home when I picked her up. As I entered her house that particular June evening, the kitchen/family room was lit only by the flickering of the TV. Because the room was dark I didn't get a good look at Ed directly, but his picture was on the TV where he was being interviewed. He had successfully negotiated a bitter contract dispute between the Philadelphia School Board and the local teachers' union. Ronnie had previously told me that her father was a professor at the Wharton School of the University of Pennsylvania; but I didn't know that he was also a federal arbitrator, the executive director for the associations of three major industries, and managed his own economic consulting business, which was engaged in studies in the United States and abroad.

My favorite amongst those studies was his work with the Philadelphia Eagles to develop the economic modeling of the financial impact that a professional sports franchise would have on a major metropolitan area. That study kept the Eagles in Philadelphia and over the years had significant ramifications for other major cities and sports franchises.

All of the above accomplishments were well underway when Ronnie and I married in the spring of 1968. Five years later, however, Ed began his most noted life's work. He invented and implemented the academic field of Entrepreneurial Studies by starting a program at the Wharton School, the first such program in the world. Eleven years later as the CEO of the Wharton Entrepreneurial Center, he faced mandatory retirement at age seventy and was very frustrated.

Ed left Wharton and switched his teaching affiliation to the Department of Political Science at Penn (the field in which he had received his PhD and which did not have mandatory retirement). A year earlier, anticipating his forced departure from Wharton, he matriculated at the University of Pennsylvania Law School, graduating at the age of seventy-two, going on to receive his Masters in Law at age seventy-five and his Doctorate of Juridical Science at age eighty-one. Having passed the Bar, he began to practice law and especially enjoyed helping Philadelphia District Attorney, Lynn Abraham, with her efforts to assist elderly victims of crime.

Just as he had been a pioneer at Wharton with his Entrepreneurial Studies, at the University of Pennsylvania Law School he enhanced the growing field of Arbitration and Alternative Dispute Resolution by endowing a Chair. An annual lectureship continues in his name.

The Thirteenth Edition of that Lecture Series was held at the University of Pennsylvania Law School on April 27, 2005. Kenneth Feinberg (Principal – The Feinberg Group, LLP, Washington, D.C. – recently well known for his appointment by President Bush to oversee the distribution of Federal funds to the families of the 9/11 victims), addressed that gathering with the following words:

"This is, of course, a bittersweet occasion. But as

the only two-time Shils Lecturer, I offer a few special words of tribute to a very special man.

We meet in an atmosphere of sorrow, but also celebration. Ed was bigger than life. His spirit – what he meant to this great University and even more importantly, his impact on family and friends – is not diminished by his death. Indeed, it is only enhanced as we pause to acknowledge the lessons that Ed taught us. His legacy pervades this room. The lessons we learned from Ed are inextricably part of our memory, providing us a blueprint for going forward with our lives.

And what are the lessons he taught us?

First, there is room for both intelligence and idealism in our public and private lives, that a liberal education is not just the way to live, but a way to live greatly. Ed's life was a healthy mixture of the practical and the idealistic.

Second, that one should be passionate about one's work, living each day as if it might be your last. Bigger than life, Ed wore his personality on his sleeve. He was an original, the real McCoy, the definitive article, marching to his own drummer. Subtlety and reticence were not part of his makeup. He always seemed to enjoy what he was doing and his exuberance was infectious. He never did anything in a small way. He believed passionately and dogged in defense of what he believed.

Finally, he added to this mixture a dose of love so profound and overwhelming that few, if any, could avoid his spell. His love of family, friends and colleagues was well known.

Wherever there is knowledge, wherever there is virtue, wherever there is passion, wherever there is love – Ed Shils will find a home, and we will use this Lecture series to celebrate Ed's legacy and remind us of his impact. Time will not wither that legacy nor dim the power of Ed's spirit – on this law school, this great university, and especially on his friends and family. His life inspires all of us to embrace the timeless virtues – compassion, generosity, and love that lie at the root of how we should live and conduct ourselves. These are the goals he stood for – and that we strive for in our mysterious never-ending journey to forge a life. In following his formula for living, we help assure the best in ourselves."

Eventually mandatory retirement was discontinued at Wharton and Ed was invited to return to teaching in the Entrepreneurial Program as Emeritus Professor. His course in Leadership was constantly oversubscribed. When Ed was eighty-eight, that course was chosen as the top course at the University of Pennsylvania.

Despite numerous awards, teaching, and accomplishments in business and consultation, his first and foremost professional passion was as mentor and guide to the thousands of students who passed through his classroom. Again and again I heard stories of his special kindnesses, the efforts that he made to support students with university jobs and/or direct financial support when necessary.

Ed's final gift to me came eight weeks before his death. As the (dynamic) Executive Director of the Dental Manufacturers of America for fifty years (1952-2002). Ed made significant academic and conceptual contributions to the dental industry. For this, he was being honored in Orlando, Florida at the American Dental Association meetings. Ronnie and I drove from Atlantic Beach to Orlando to spend an overnight.

The first edition of "When I Became A Psychiatrist..." had been published a number of months prior to Ed's passing. I was surprised when during our last breakfast together he turned to me and said, "You know, I read your book again. It is really good. It has helped me to understand health and medicine in a new way. You have to do something with it."

There had never been a doubt in my mind that there would be a second edition. However, my daily life is often so busy that I had been procrastinating. It was Ed's enthusiasm that got the ball rolling again.

If I were to identify the most important idea in "Main Street" it would be the notion of inherited affective bandwidth. The upside of that bandwidth is affective enrichment, a gift that not all people receive. Ed had this in spades.

Kaye Redfield Jamison's most recent book entitled "Exuberance" deals with grace and eloquence about the world of affective enrichment. One particular passage from Dr. Jamison's book struck me as being particularly descriptive of Edward Shils. "I believe that exuberance is incomparably more important that we acknowledge. If, as it had been claimed, enthusiasm finds the opportunity and energy makes the most of them, a mood of mind that yokes the two is formidable indeed. Exuberant people take in the world and act upon it differently than those who are less lively and less energetically engaged. They hold their ideas with passion and delight, and they act upon them with love and dispatch. Their love of life and of adventure palpable." That was Ed.

CONTENTS

PREFACE

Many people, including some physicians, just
don't understand psychiatry. I became all too
aware of this when I switched to psychiatry after
years of family practice and emergency medicine.

At its best, psychiatry's core is the mystery of our
humanness. It is not some eccentric abstraction that
denotes craziness or weakness; nor is it a repository
for patients whose problems seem to have no obvious answers. The condescending phrase, "It's all in
your head" makes me crazy (excuse the expression).
With all due respect, and with as much sophistication as our ignorance will allow, it may not be all in
our heads; however, in a very real and positive sense,
much of it is.

PART I

LISA

·· 1 ··

THE BEACH

Sometimes when I'm running, I leave the earth. I don't know where I was that particular morning, but the footsteps behind me brought me back. I smiled to myself. A few years earlier I would have played the game, no looking around, just subtle acceleration until I knew the other person was no longer gaining. But the passage of time and my aging hamstrings have stolen even the modest speed I once had.

The steps drew closer. I still didn't look until I heard a quiet voice just behind my right shoulder. "Hey Carl."

In Vermont everyone said "hi." Since moving to Florida four years ago it had become "hey." Feels friendlier.

I turned. At the exact moment that I recognized Lisa Brady, the orange edge of the rising sun sliced the horizon.

"Hey Lisa," a brief pause, "isn't this gorgeous?" I intended to describe the ocean sunrise but as I was speaking realized that the words were very appropriate for her.

"Breathtaking," she said, "and it happens every day."

I smiled. Our steps struck the sand in unison as a warm breeze pushed gently from the south. She made no effort to pass me.

I didn't know Lisa well. We'd been introduced on a few occasions by her husband Ben, a fellow morning exerciser at the gym. A few months back Ben and I had discovered our mutual Philadelphia roots, and that shifted our relationship a little beyond "how are you?" We also had something else in common. Ben and Lisa work together; in fact I had just noticed their sign in Sawgrass Village, "Brady and Brady, Attorneys at Law." I took special note of that because my wife Ronnie is a psychologist and we also share our professional lives.

As the sun rose our pace quickened; I thought Lisa pushed, she probably thought it was me.

"Ben tells me you're a psychiatrist."

I nodded. "Uh huh."

"And you also have a law degree?"

I nodded again.

"But you don't practice law?"

"That's right, never took the Bar."

After a few more seconds she continued her

questioning. "Where'd you go to law school?"

We had been running along the edge of the water. The tide was coming in and at that moment both of us had to move slightly to the left to avoid one of the precocious waves that is first to reach higher ground. As the water receded I answered, "Berkeley."

"Good school."

"Yep — how about you, where'd you go?"

"Penn," she answered.

"Good school."

She looked at me and we smiled; there was an easy humor between us. We chatted and then ran silent for a minute or two and had almost reached the Ponte Vedra Inn when Lisa spoke again, "I've got to head back but I wanted to ask you something." She paused as though she needed permission to continue. I had a hunch what she was about to say.

"Sure."

"I've never seen any kind of counselor before, but I think I could talk to you. There are a few things that have been bothering me — could I make an appointment sometime?"

"No."

Lisa looked startled. I remained serious for a split second, then began to smile. Her face assumed a mask of mock anger, then she smiled back. We ran another fifty yards before reaching the first building of the Inn. She turned slightly toward me, "I'll call your office."

"My office manager's name is Dawn. I'll let her know you'll be calling."

"Thanks." As Lisa turned back she gave a little wave.

I waved in return and continued to run north.

·· 2 ··

TEARS FOR "NO REASON"

My office colleagues have given me an Indian nickname; they call me "Running Late." By the end of a long day (or even a short one for that matter), I'm often behind schedule. This evening was no exception. It was 8:20 when I poked my head into the waiting room. Lisa was stunning in a pair of jeans and a white blouse.

"Hey, Lisa, I'm sorry I'm late."

She didn't let me explain. "No problem," she said as she stood up.

I walked from the waiting room to my office and she followed. I stopped and waited for her to enter the room first. She stood for a few moments and looked around, which in itself is a sign of health. So many who walk into this room have too much discomfort to notice anything but their pain.

Before sitting on the couch, Lisa walked to the windows. The scene outside was "Florida Pastoral," a soft green manicured expanse of golf course. It was twilight and the sky was cloudless, a luminescent Maxfield Parish blue. "This is lovely."

"Some evenings it's truly magic," I said.

Lisa continued to stand at the window, lost in thought. I quietly sat and after a few moments she noticed and moved to the couch. For the first time she didn't seem comfortable. "I suddenly feel a little silly."

"Why?"

"I guess I grew up thinking that you had to be crazy to see a psychiatrist." I nodded. She was trying to sound humorous but she was a bit embarrassed and blushed slightly.

"I know exactly what you mean. People have the strangest ideas as to what goes on in a psychiatrist's office — but it's really the same kind of help I provided for many patients when I was a family doctor."

"You were a family doctor?"

"Uh huh."

"Really?"

"Really." I smiled. The hour was late, no one was waiting and I felt very relaxed. "Would you like to hear a true story? It's related to your uncomfortable feelings."

"I love stories." Now Lisa was smiling.

"Once upon a time I sort of left psychiatry."

"What do you mean?"

"Well — years ago, I was an emergency physician. Even during my psychiatry training I continued practicing emergency medicine in San Francisco."

"You trained in San Francisco?"

"Yes." I paused, but there were no further questions. "When I finished my residency and started my psychiatric practice, I had many referrals, not necessarily because I was a good psychiatrist but because colleagues trusted me as an emergency doc." She nodded. "But, I didn't feel comfortable. I finished my training with the feeling that there was supposed to be a right way to do therapy — that there was a kind of emotional neutrality – a reserve that was expected, which to me didn't feel natural."

Lisa was nodding. "I've heard that some psychiatrists don't really talk."

"That was more true a few years back, but it's still a bit that way."

"And here you are telling me a story."

"Yep." We both smiled.

"Anyway, as a new psychiatrist I would sit hour after hour, in my Fillmore Street office, uncertain that I was really helping. I was becoming disenchanted with my new specialty." Lisa was nodding, definitely interested.

"At about that same time my wife Ronnie was finishing her Ph.D. in clinical psychology."

Lisa suddenly had a funny look. "Ronnie?"

"Yes."

"Did she ever teach aerobics?"

"She used to."

"I used to take classes from her. I thought she was very good."

"Thanks. I'll tell her."

"And she works with you?"

"Yes, she does."

"Kind of like Ben and me."

"Very similar."

"Interesting."

We were both silent for a few seconds and I continued. "It was about the time I finished my training that our son Eli was born. As a father I found myself thinking more about family and East Coast roots. Then out of the blue a physician friend in Vermont called to tell me about an opportunity in family practice."

"Didn't he know you had gone into psychiatry?"

"I think he did, and that's what's strange. I remember laughing, saying 'I should move from San Francisco to Vermont and go back to family medicine?'. A year later we were in Bennington."

"You closed your psychiatry practice in San Francisco and returned to family practice in Vermont?"

"Strange but true. In the spring of 1980 we moved from San Francisco to Bennington and joined a family practice. It seemed like an ideal situation for me and ideal for Ronnie as well because she would become the on-site psychologist."

"But you would be a family doctor?"

"Yes. But so much of family medicine is psychiatry anyway that I thought my training would serve me well."

"So how is it that you returned to psychiatry?"

"Well, what happened was probably predictable. When I arrived in town, Bennington had only two psychiatrists. There was really a need for more, and my medical colleagues began to make requests for psychiatric consultations. 'Would you see this patient in the hospital?' 'Couldn't you see this young woman, I think she really needs help?' Eventually I found myself practicing psychiatry in the morning and family medicine in the afternoon. Inevitably, medical emergencies would occur in the morning while I was counseling and psychiatric emergencies would occur in the afternoon while I was seeing general medical patients."

"So what happened?"

"It dawned on me that I was enjoying psychiatry. I had given up some of the formality that was the legacy of my training." I smiled. "If I hadn't, I probably wouldn't be telling you this story."

Lisa was nodding.

" I had begun to work more from the heart and it felt better. Also, Ronnie and I enjoyed working together and especially doing therapy with other couples. So, with much discussion and a lot of soul searching we decided to open our own office; Ronnie would continue doing what she was doing and I would return to full time psychiatry. Life would be simpler. I could focus."

"What about your family practice patients?"

"In early September of 1981 I sent a letter to all of my family practice patients and as much as possible I spoke to everyone. I tried to help everyone find a new doctor."

"How did they feel?"

"Most understood, but it wasn't easy." Lisa nodded. "But what I didn't realize was that in making the switch, I'd inadvertently created a social experiment in community attitude."

"How?"

"Because I was already a psychiatrist I was literally able to change my specialty overnight. On Friday, October 23, 1981, I was a family doctor in a small town. On Monday, October 26th, I was a psychiatrist in the same small town. And what happened hovered somewhere between sad and humorous."

"What do you mean?"

"In the weeks before the changeover, when I would walk down Main Street as a family doctor, I was constantly greeted with 'Hi, Doc, how ya' doing?'. Sometimes people would wave or shout from across the street; there was a very friendly feeling. But as soon as I officially became a psychiatrist, the difference was dramatic; I would walk down Main Street and no one waved. I mean no one waved. And if I was greeted verbally, it was only when someone passed at a close distance and said hello with a quiet voice. Even lips seemed not to move. I would smile, thinking the whole town had learned ventriloquism. No one ever shouted 'Hey Doc' any more."

Lisa was contemplative, shaking her head almost imperceptibly.

We sat in silence for a few moments. Finally I asked softly, "So, how can I help?"

In response to my question, Lisa's eyes became moist. She took a tissue from the box always available next to the sofa, "This is so silly — I have no idea why I'm crying." She looked away for a few seconds and then returned her gaze, "I'm here because sometimes I'm not really happy — and I do this, I suddenly cry and it doesn't make sense." Blotting her eyes, she took a deep breath.

•• 3 ••

LOST CUSTODY

I remained quiet as she took a second tissue. After a little more dabbing she continued. "I mean there's no reason for me to be unhappy. Ben's a great guy and David's a wonderful little boy. I am pretty happy with my work and we don't have any financial worries — I've just got nothing to be unhappy about."

"But you are unhappy?"

"Sometimes... but more often I'm not really unhappy — but I'm not happy either."

"Out of sorts?"

"Maybe a little."

"And this is how you usually feel?"

"No." Lisa was thoughtful for a few moments. "I'm not really sure — isn't that funny? It's not the majority of my life, but these moods are familiar enough that I realize I don't pay too much attention if I'm a little down." She hesitated and looked at me, "You know when I saw you running on the beach the other morning, I really wasn't sure whether to make an appointment, but somehow after a few miles it seemed like a good idea."

I nodded. The room was quiet and Lisa conveyed no sense of urgency. After waiting a few more moments, I said, "Can I ask you a few questions?"

"Sure."

"I assume you're sort of flat now?"

"I guess you could say that."

"Well, you describe — how are you feeling?"

"I don't know — not really enthusiastic about much."

"How about work?"

"Oh — it's okay. But I have to force myself to get things done."

I paused. "Are you sleeping well?"

"Not really."

"Trouble falling asleep?"

"Not so much falling asleep, but I get up a few times during the night. And when it gets to be four or five, if I'm up I can't go back to sleep."

"And that's also not like you normally?"

"I'm a pretty light sleeper, especially if David gets up. I hear him immediately — but usually I sleep pretty well."

"David is your son?"

"Yes."

"How old is he?"

"Just turned six."

"Any other children?"

"No, he's the one and only. He is definitely the light of my life — our lives, but now even with David sometimes I just want him to leave me alone, and that's not like me."

I jotted a few notes. Then continued, "You've had these feelings before?"

"Yes."

"Have you ever experienced a time before when you've felt kind of like you've been feeling recently?"

"Yes."

"And you've never seen anybody?"

"You mean like a psychiatrist?"

"A psychiatrist, a psychologist, a counselor."

"No, I never did. The idea of doing something, of seeing someone, has floated through my mind – but I was hesitant like I mentioned on the beach – seeing a psychiatrist is not what everybody does." She smiled, "I also assumed that my moodiness was a normal part of life."

"To some degree I agree with you; it really is."

"So if that's the case, why am I here now?"

"Good question." I became quiet and waited while Lisa was thinking.

"It's because I've just felt particularly rotten lately and Ben told me that you seemed like a nice guy.

"So Ben knows you've come to see me?"

"Uh huh – he thought it was fine."

"Good." There was a pause and I continued. "So why do you think you feel particularly rotten lately? Is there anything happening in your life now or in the past few months that has been particularly stressful?"

"The only thing that comes to mind is a very difficult case that I finished a few weeks ago. We lost and it was upsetting."

"Ben mentioned you practice family law."

"Yes."

"Was that the context of this case?"

"Yes. I represented the husband in a divorce. I like him. I think he's a good person, devoted to his children, a son who is eight and a little girl who is six. I realize I can't be objective because he's my client, but I don't like his wife. She seems punitive and mean spirited. It seemed clear to me that the children wanted to be with their father, but the judge…," she hesitated. "Anyway, we lost and I hate to say this, but the judge in the case happens to be a woman who has fairly young children herself. I know her." Silence again.

"So the wife got custody?"

"Yes, despite strong testimony supporting my client."

"And you felt as though the judge's own personal situation led her to be more sympathetic to the wife."

"I did."

I smiled. "You know if there's one thing I learned in law school, it's that the law is not what it seems to be. Everyone thinks it's so precise and logical, but it's not. It's really so psychological, so responsive to intangibles – the state trooper who likes your looks and gives you a warning instead of a ticket, a juror who can't stand the tone of voice of a defendant, or," I nodded slightly towards Lisa as I said, "the feelings of a female judge who has her own young children."

"So that's what you learned in law school?" Lisa was smiling.

"That's about all I remember," I smiled back.

"Well, to a large extent I think you're right." She turned her face slightly towards the window and the vanishing twilight, momentarily lost in thought. I waited. She turned back, but was silent.

I asked, "What did Ben think about your custody case?"

"Ben tried to be helpful." She deepened her voice to imitate her husband, "You just can't win them all, you did your best." He was sweet and I appreciate it, but somehow it didn't make me feel any better."

"Do you think if the same case had happened a

year earlier, or even a few months earlier, it would
have bothered you in the same way?"

"That's a very interesting question – I've never
thought about that. This is not the first time I've
lost and it won't be the last time, so why did it both-
er me so much?" Lisa became silent; she moved her
hand to her lips and rubbed her lower lip with her
little finger. "I felt that this case was particularly
unfair, but I think you're suggesting that I was
already a little depressed or sensitive when I was
dealing with it – maybe without realizing it?"

"Maybe."

"Maybe?" Lisa smiled. "I thought doctors
knew everything."

"Maybe." I laughed. So did she.

··4··

NORMAL?

I purposely schedule many first visits at the end of the day so I don't feel rushed; having the time to really talk is very important. Since we started late I asked, "Are you pressed for time?"

Lisa shook her head. "No, not at all. Ben's at home with David and I'm in no hurry." As if to punctuate the point she slipped off her shoes and tucked her feet under her on the sofa.

I continued, "Even though we may talk for a while, by the time you leave here tonight I'm sure there will be a lot I won't know about you and your family." She was nodding. "But I would appreciate it if you would help me understand as much as possible of your perspective."

"Sure."

"So — what was your family like when you were growing up? Supportive? Harsh?

In any way abusive?"

Lisa didn't hesitate, "Loving, I am very lucky —

I have great parents."

"What's your mom like?"

"My mother is terrific. She seems to handle everything with ease and is always there for us. I've always felt loved."

"Was she always at home?"

"She had been a teacher before she married, but after I was born she didn't return to teaching."

"And your dad?"

"The most difficult thing about Dad was that he traveled so much. He was an executive with an oil company and until I was fifteen we lived mostly in Brazil and Argentina."

"So you're bilingual?"

"Trilingual actually; Brazilians speak Portuguese and Argentineans speak Spanish."

"I didn't remember that Portuguese was the language of Brazil."

"Si."

I smiled.

"Sometimes I hardly saw Dad, especially when we were living in Argentina. But most of the time when he was around he was fun."

"Most of the time?"

"Occasionally he got upset — I'm not sure that I knew exactly why — I assumed that it was in relation to his business."

"How upset?"

"Grumpy — sour — angry on the phone; but the clouds would pass pretty quickly."

"So you don't think that either of your parents has a significant tendency to be moody or depressed?"

Lisa thought for a moment. "Not really. Certainly not Mom. And Dad – well, maybe he was slightly that way when he was irritable, but I think he's pretty much an even-tempered guy."

"And you never saw your mom in a down time?"

"I can't say that. A few years back she went through a slump, probably around menopause, but I don't think she was ever seriously depressed." Lisa hesitated — "Come to think of it, I recently had a friend who had post-partum depression. I was talking with Mom and she told me she had been pretty depressed for awhile after Bill was born."

"Bill's your brother?"

"Yes."

"Do you have other siblings?"

"A sister."

"Younger or older?"

"Both Bill and Jane are younger. I'm thirty-seven, Jane is thirty-five, and Bill just turned thirty-two."

"Do you get along?"

"Jane and I had our battles when we were

growing up, but we're best friends now. Maybe because Bill was the boy and was five years younger — somehow he and I never had a lot of conflict, and we've enjoyed each other even more as we've gotten older."

"So you were about five when your mother had her post-partum problem?"

"That's right."

"Do you know how long the depression lasted?"

"Not really. It was a surprise when she told me. And if she hadn't been moody around menopause, I couldn't even imagine her being down."

"Because she was so up most of the time?"

"Exactly."

"So all in all there aren't a lot of deep, dark secrets that come from your childhood?"

"Sorry — unless I'm amnesic, there are no skeletons in the closet."

"Are your parents still in South America?"

"Oh no. Once we returned to the states, to corporate headquarters in New Jersey, they never went back."

"All in all, sounds like you had an interesting childhood."

"I was lucky."

"You were." We both smiled.

"What about you, Lisa — what were you like?"

1   "What do you mean?"

    "Well – sort of paint a broad brushstroke emotional portrait of yourself as a young person."

    "You mean when I was a teenager?"

5   "Sure, and even before."

    Lisa sat quietly for a few moments. "I was pretty happy as a little girl, maybe overly sensitive. If someone said something that I thought was a criticism, I felt terrible. If I thought I didn't do something right, I became very upset — I would cry easily."

    "So you were hard on yourself?"

    "Always."

    "Even today?"

15   "I guess so. Sometimes maybe a little more — sometimes less."

    "Would you call yourself moody?"

    "I guess I was moody as a teenager."

    "But not when you were younger?"

20   She hesitated. "I don't think so, but I'm not sure."

    I nodded. "What about now?"

    "You mean have I been moody recently?"

    "Yes."

25   "I guess you could say that."

    "And lately you've been down?"

    "Pretty much."

    "How are you doing at work?"

"I'm just kind of forcing myself to get things done. That's not like me."

"What is like you?"

"I'm usually pretty motivated and interested in my cases. I don't procrastinate. But when I'm down, like now, I often come smack against a court appearance or a deposition before I can get going."

"Sounds like you're feeling a little guilty about that."

"Uh huh." She was nodding unconsciously.

"Have you been feeling sad?"

"A little."

"Irritable?"

She hesitated. "Maybe you'd better ask Ben — I don't think I've been particularly bitchy."

"Anxious?"

"At times."

"Do you worry?"

"Do I worry?" She smiled. "That's almost a joke. I've always been the family worrier."

"Can't get your mind off something you start thinking about?"

"I can be sort of obsessed."

"Is that worse lately?"

She hesitated, then nodded.

"How's your energy level?"

"Lousy."

"I know your sleep is interrupted." She nodded.

"So I assume you don't feel rested when you wake up in the morning?"

"That's right, not lately."

"Concentrating well?"

"Not lately."

"Have you ever felt bad enough at any point that it really didn't seem like it was worth living?"

"Have I ever thought about suicide?"

"Yes."

Lisa shook her head, a hint of a sad smile darkened her pretty face and she shrugged. "On a few occasions I've wondered what it would be like if I weren't here, but I really believe I wouldn't ever do anything like that."

"So you never made any plans to do yourself in?"

"No. Those thoughts were really fleeting." Lisa waited a few seconds and then asked, "So am I pretty depressed?"

I shook my head no.

She seemed surprised. "I'm not depressed?"

"I didn't say that. You're just not severely depressed. But for the moment let's forget the word depression; it's confusing."

"Why is 'depression' confusing?"

"I'll explain, but first let me see if I'm on the right track."

"Okay."

"Beside the recent custody case, is there anything else that's going on now that is really bothering you?"

"Maybe there's something I'm not aware of, but there's not a hint of any significant problem, not even many insignificant problems."

"As you said, you are very fortunate."

"I appreciate that, and that's in part why it's taken me so long to talk about this. It doesn't make sense that I feel depressed sometimes."

"If everything were logical I'd be out of business."

She smiled.

"But I'm glad you decided to finally talk about how you feel."

"I am too." She smiled again in a more wistful way.

"From what you've said and how you seem, I'll describe what I think is going on — and you tell me if I'm accurate."

"Sure."

"My guess is that at times like this in the past you've always managed to function. Even at your worst, you go to work and get through the day, you do what you have to, but you're a little...." I thought for a moment, "— there's no joie de 'vivre." Lisa began to nod. I noticed her eyes had become moist again. I continued, "It's like going through the motions — it's okay but dull."

"Um huh."

"If the joke is really good you can laugh, but the easy spontaneity that you feel at other times is missing?"

Lisa glanced at me and looked away. She reached for the Kleenex box, took a tissue, and dabbed her eyes.

"So I'm on the right track?"

She nodded again.

"But I bet it's only part of the picture."

"What do you mean?"

"No one comes to see me for the first time and says 'Doc I'm feeling terrific and I just can't stand it'." She smiled. "People come in when they're down — depressed, if we have to use that word. But over the years I've probably made more mistakes by not asking questions about the better times."

"The better times?"

"Yes. For example, I would suspect there have been times — days, hours, weeks, when you have felt terrific. When your personal sky is quite blue. When you're full of energy, creative, just raring to go."

"You're absolutely right."

"The way you feel now is sort of like treading water, and the way you've felt at those better times has almost been like," I hesitated," dancing on the waves?"

Lisa laughed. "That is so accurate it's uncanny."

"I'm glad you feel like I understand."

"But I still want to know what you meant when you said that 'depression' is confusing"

"I think the word depression is somewhat misleading, unfortunately at times even contributing to a misunderstanding of mental health."

"How?"

"Suppose you ask everyone at a symphony or a football game if they've ever been depressed — what do you think most people would say?"

She thought for a moment. "Probably most people would say they've been depressed at one time or another."

"I think that's absolutely right. Almost everyone will say they've been depressed at some time — but many will actually not have experienced the kind of feelings that you and I are talking about. And certainly not the intense anguish and paralysis that takes hold of some people."

"So some people who think they've been depressed really wouldn't understand how others feel."

"That's right. I'm not sure what word I would substitute that would be better. The Eskimos have some phenomenal number of words for snow. Maybe we should have more for moods. Some people who are very even tempered may experience some minor ups and downs, but nothing really extreme. I believe they don't really understand someone who has had more significant depression because they haven't really stood in those shoes. And that's not a criticism in any way; but I believe that many emotionally comfortable people think that individuals who cannot take their feelings in hand and just control them have some kind of character flaw or are weak-willed."

Lisa was nodding. "And you don't think that's true?"

"No. Definitely not."

Lisa became quiet, thoughtful. I waited and when she said nothing further I slightly shifted gears.

"Have you ever had a time before this when you've experienced a time before this when you've felt kind of like what you have been feeling lately?"

"Definitely — not that often, but as I think about it there have been other blue periods.... — As I said, I just figured my moods were a normal part of life."

"And I mostly agree with you."

"So again, why am I here?"

"I think you're here because you feel that your quality of life is not what you think it should be. You've had those thoughts for a while, but psychiatry was too much associated with the idea of being weak or crazy to cross an invisible moat that surrounds my office. I'm really a quality of life physician, not a 'crazy' doctor."

She raised her eyebrows and said, "I won't even go there."

"You know what I mean."

"I do. — So you really think I'm normal?"

"I really do. Being a little down or even moderately down makes you a little depressed or moderately depressed, but not abnormal. Does a normal person see a cardiologist, a hematologist, a neurologist, an internist…?"

"I see where you're going."

"The problem is again with the distortions related to psychiatry. With other medical illnesses, the person is not stigmatized with the notion that they somehow are abnormal because they have a medical problem. The medical problem is part of normal existence, but it's certainly not ideal. Is a cold normal?" I answered myself, "Sure, it's normal in the sense that it's naturally occurring and commonly within the realm of human experience. But it's not ideal. High blood pressure, anemia, arthritis are all arguably a normal part of the human condition, and the people who have these problems are also considered normal people."

"That's really a liberating way to think about things."

"I'm glad it feels that way."

Lisa was abruptly silent, brow furrowed, then she said, "Ironically maybe there is a benefit to depression, which certain other non-ideal situations don't have."

"What do you mean?"

"I don't see very much redeeming value in having high blood pressure or diabetes, even though I might agree that it's not necessarily abnormal to experience those things. But maybe depression has some value. Assuming someone is not intensely depressed, not suicidal, might there be some benefit to the 'normal' struggle with mild depression — by strengthening someone's ability to persevere and grow in the face of adversity?"

"You feel that's your situation?"

"I think it may be. Nobody wants tough times, but often you learn from them."

I probably sighed. "Lisa, you don't know how much I've thought about this. It's ironic that so many people who have never experienced more than an occasional mild down day have the idea that those of us who become more depressed lack character or willpower. Ironically, I do think that some depression can be a real character builder."

"So where do you draw the line? When do you treat?"

"Obviously, if the depression involves the real

risk of suicide, I would try to be very persuasive and
insistent about treatment; but in a situation like
yours, I think it's more a personal choice. It's a cost-
benefit sort of thing. Without treatment you would
lead a normal life. With treatment you would lead
a normal life."

"But normal would be a qualitatively different
experience in each of those two situations?"

"Yes."

·· 5 ··

CHICKEN OR EGG?

L isa seemed almost relieved, then she became quiet again. I waited. Finally, she said, "Could I ask you about something you said before?"

"Sure, what's that?"

"You asked me if Henry Pryor's custody case had happened a few months earlier would I have been as upset."

"Yes?"

"Were you implying that didn't actually cause my depression — that I might already have been a little depressed at the time that I lost the case?"

"I was at least raising that possibility." I hesitated, "It was Henry's divorce you were referring to?"

She asked me, "You know him?"

"Both him and Marilyn, and I understand...." I stopped mid sentence. I was too late. "You don't like Marilyn?"

I smiled. "I didn't say that."

Lisa raised her eyebrows and simply said, "Oh." She graciously remained silent.

After a few awkward seconds I said, "Getting back to what we were discussing, in hindsight it often becomes apparent that depression that seemed to be caused by stress had already begun before the stress."

"So what seemed so stressful wouldn't have felt that way if the person hadn't been depressed in the first place?"

"Right."

She thought for a moment, "Are you also implying that there are probably times when we're more susceptible to the effects of stress?"

"Yes. So often someone has told me they were depressed because of something that happened; weeks or months later they realized that the boss or whatever hadn't been the problem — it was their down mood at the time which made a mountain out of a molehill."

"So it's a chicken or egg situation; which comes first, the depression or the circumstance?"

"Exactly! And that chicken or egg confusion is the crux of what is often so misunderstood about mental health."

"What do you mean?"

"I mean we're dealing with an area of health that is labeled psychological, but it is crucially impacted by our built in genetically influenced physiology." I hesitated. "I'm not implying that psychology is unimportant; this is not an either/or situation! But the more experience I have, the more convinced I've become that the practice of psychiatry is no different than my former family practice in terms of its medical foundation."

"When you say medical foundation you are referring to chemistry?"

"Well, chemistry is a big part of the problem, but I can't say too often that it's not just chemistry – It's not an either/or situation. I am very respectful of the part that stress plays, but I believe that psychological stress provokes different chemical changes in different individuals. If you have four different people in the same sort of emotionally charged situation, one may develop an ulcer, another person may have an arthritis flare, the third asthma, and the fourth may start the road to a depressive episode. The specific problem that each of us develops is determined by the body we inherit. It's actually the ease of 'provokability' of a particular part of our body machinery that defines what health problems each of us is likely to have."

Lisa was quiet; I could almost 'see' her wheels turning. "Basically you are talking about this notion that mental illness is caused by a chemical imbalance in the brain."

"Right. But this is not really a revelation. Just about every medical problem that I've ever treated has some relationship to chemical imbalance."

"What do you mean?"

"What is required to have diabetes?"

"Too much sugar in the blood?"

"That's correct, but what really is the cause of that improper amount of sugar?"

"Something to do with insulin?"

"That's usually true, but what I'm getting at is that it is a chemical imbalance in the sugar regulating system which leads to diabetes."

"Hmm."

"So what is required in order to have an ulcer?"

"A chemical imbalance?"

"Bingo. And what is required for rheumatoid arthritis?"

"A chemical imbalance."

"Absolutely right. What about lupus or gout?"

"Chemical imbalance."

"Like I said, I cannot think of many medical problems that in one way or another are not related to a chemical imbalance in some system in the body. It's not that we simply inherit all medical problems per se, we inherit a kind of sensitivity or as I said 'provokability' in our sugar regulating chemistry, or our blood pressure chemistry — or in the case of depression or anxiety or mania, in our mood regulating chemistry."

"Interesting — what about the common cold? That's not a chemical imbalance. Isn't that caused by a virus?"

"Yes and no."

"Yes and no?"

"Yep." I smiled.

"You're kidding me."

"No. I'm not kidding. I'll explain about colds, but first let me explain the bigger picture, at least as I see it."

"Okay."

I placed my spread hand over my chest. "This body is our health system. Day and night, it operates automatically to take care of us. It operates very well the majority of the time. But each of us inherits a few parts of this machine that are less than ideal. For those less efficient parts, we use our increasing medical knowledge to make necessary adjustments. Okay so far?"

"Uh huh."

"So this unique body that each of us has is comprised of different physiologic pieces, all of which have different functions and produce different chemicals."

"Like a puzzle?"

"That's a good way of looking at it. But I would say it's more like a symphony orchestra, because the pieces don't just fit together, they work in a very interrelated way."

She nodded.

"So let's suppose that instead of using the word chemicals that our body is producing, we substitute the word drugs."

"By drugs you mean hormones or...?"

"Hormones, enzymes, digestive juices, neurotransmitters — whatever."

"Okay. I see what you mean."

"So we can look at this machine we inherit as a drug manufacturing company. I don't know precisely how many drugs we each manufacture, but the brain alone manufactures more than five hundred different chemicals. Each area of our body, each piece of our orchestra, manufactures its own set of drugs for its particular function."

"Okay."

"Now — Imagine that each part of our body has its own group of internal physicians who manage and prescribe the drugs produced there."

A slight smile began to play around the corners of Lisa's mouth.

"Maybe ninety-five percent of the time, maybe ninety-eight percent of the time our internal manufacturing and our internal prescribing is ideal. But with each of us inevitably there are a few parts of our body in which the manufacturing or prescribing may be slightly off. And with each of us, the parts that are misfiring are not necessarily the same. With one person it's the digestive system, with another it's the immune system, with another it's the cardiovascular system, with another it's the mood system."

Lisa nodded, indicating her understanding.

"Whether it's through the use of talk therapy, light therapy, medication, herbs, diet, exercise, acupuncture, homeopathy, prayer, massage, meditation, hypnosis, or voodoo, healers of different cultures all over the world are really trying to adjust those parts of our magnificent machine that don't work quite right. In a very real way, any physician or healer is collaborating with this internal health system. For example, antibiotics have been responsible for the greatest statistical improvement in the health of populations around the world. When I prescribe an antibiotic, I know it will not likely work without the cooperation of the immune system of the patient. Without that immune system antibiotics are sycophants flailing in a vacuum."

"Sycophants flailing in a vacuum?"

I laughed. "I get carried away, but the point I'm making is that even with the use of antibiotics, treatment of infection would often fail without the participation of the body's own immune chemistry. Okay?"

"Yep."

"It's also very important to realize that some
people can fight certain infections without antibiotics, while others can't. The intensity of the infection is one component of the equation, but the
intrinsic inherited ability of an individual's immune
system to function efficiently is definitely the other
part. And that's where the cold comes in. We are all
exposed to cold viruses. So it's certainly possible
that in certain situations or because of certain occu-
pations, some of us are exposed much more. But it
always fascinated me as a family doctor that some
of my patients said they never got colds while others would get four to six colds a year. I am very certain that those who tended to get fewer colds were
not better at dodging viruses that those who got
many colds."

Lisa nodded.

"The difference from one person to the next in
all likelihood is the difference between the chemical
function of their immune systems. With something
as common as cold viruses, the major issue is one's
ability to fight the virus, not whether we're ever
exposed."

"Got it."

"And even though we may overcome or prevent
a cold episode, we haven't changed our inherited
susceptibility to colds in general. By taking vitamins, or herbs, or meditating, or whatever, we may

temporarily improve immune function; but when we stop taking those chemicals or doing those activities, our susceptibility to colds tends to return to what it was before."

Lisa nodded.

"Let's suppose we lived in a peculiar world and I was still a family doctor and you came to me and said, 'I wonder if you could help me develop an ulcer for a few months?'"

She raised her eyebrows.

"Anyway, depending on your family history and personal background, I might have to say, 'I'm really sorry but I can't help you. There's probably nothing that would provoke your particular digestive drugs to dysregulate — to go out of balance. Excessive alcohol or high stress or the use of caffeine or spices, or exposure of the intestines to certain bacteria might provoke someone else's system, which is more sensitive or vulnerable than yours, to develop an ulcer, but unfortunately your digestive drug manufacturing plant and your internal gastroenterologist are just too good. You can't have an ulcer, Mrs. Brady, I'm truly sorry.'" I smiled. "I know that's sort of ridiculous, but do I make my point?"

"Uh huh. Some parts of our machine work so well that despite various kinds of stress and improper health habits, nothing is likely to go wrong; at the

same time, there are other parts which may be very
vulnerable or sensitive and easily go out of balance."

"Exactly — and we don't have a damn thing to
do about what is vulnerable and what is built like
the Rock of Gibraltar. And neither do our parents.
It's really a genetic crapshoot. Until genetic treatment becomes available, all we can do is to be as
intelligent as possible and figure out who we are as
individuals. We discover our own vulnerabilities
and then we tweak them as best we can."

Lisa was very quiet.

"Am I still making sense?"

She nodded, "Yes. Very much so."

"Good." I hesitated, "Speaking of health Lisa,
how is yours?"

"You mean in general?"

"Yes."

"As far as I know it's fine."

"Are you taking any medications?"

"No."

"Do you have any allergies to medication or
anything else?"

"Nope." She was thoughtful for a moment.
"I'm pretty healthy; no medical problems at all
except maybe this mild depression, if I'm understanding what you're saying."

Blue Genes

"I think you do understand."

"Good, but I'm bothered by one thing."

"Just one thing?"

"I'll think of more," she smiled, "but for now one thing."

"Which is?"

"The issue of genes. What I mean is — as I look at my family, it is not filled with mental illness."

I gave her a look.

"Oops — I mean quality of life problems."

"That's better, but let me help you with your approach to this. When you think about your family, I'd like you to do a couple of things."

"Which are?"

"First, take a very broad overview; look not only at your parents and brothers and sisters, but also at your grandparents, your aunts, uncles, cousins, nieces, nephews — all of your biological relatives on both your mother's and father's sides. Perhaps you've had no relatives who have been diagnosed with a so-called mental health problem or took medication. But there may be some relatives, especially distant ones, who have been treated and you wouldn't know about it."

"True."

"Take yourself as an example. You've always been somewhat moody and sensitive, but I don't describe you as crazy or mentally ill; you've always been able to function appropriately, although at times you undoubtedly operate better than at other times. So if someone else in your family were asked to say what family members may have some sort of difficulty, you probably wouldn't be included. Right?"

"Hmm. I guess so."

"What I would like you to do is to look at your family in a more intuitive way. I'm looking for patterns of temperament and mood that seem to run in the family. We sometimes get too caught up by diagnostic pigeonholes. There's a definite utility in giving problems a name, but people don't always fit into nice neat diagnostic packages. So, as you look at your family panorama, let your intuition reign. Are there relatives who may have a tendency, like yourself, to be sensitive or moody? Or relatives who seem to be very high strung, low strung, or are

always worried? Or are always upbeat, or unusual-
ly negative, or irritable? In other words, I'm not just
looking for someone who has a formal diagnosis."

"I understand. But as you were talking, I did
realize that there is at least one person in my family who has been formally diagnosed."

"Who's that?"

"My aunt, my mother's sister; she's been diagnosed as manic-depressive. Now it's called bipolar?"

"Right."

"I probably didn't get to know her as well as I
would have if I had grown up in the States. But I've
always liked her."

"Any other relatives in your mom's family that
you know of who had any kind of difficulty?"

"Well, my grandfather, mom's dad, was a 'character' — always a bit eccentric." She smiled. "He
was a toy maker."

"But as far as you know he didn't have any sort
of formal treatment for anything?"

"I don't think he did; he died quite some time
ago when I was a teenager, and I doubt very much
that he ever saw a doctor or took any medication
related to what we're talking about. I doubt that he
actually had to."

"Anyone else?"

"Well, now that I think about it my first cousin,
my aunt's daughter, was hospitalized for postpar-

tum depression last year after she had her baby."

"Was she the daughter of your aunt who is bipolar?"

"Yes." Lisa hesitated, thoughtful, then she said quietly almost to herself, "Interesting." After a few quiet moments I continued. "What about your father's family?"

"You know, I said Dad wasn't depressed, but he does have that tendency at times to be moody, but not in any extreme way." A little smile appeared on Lisa's face. "I guess I could almost be describing myself." I nodded as she allowed that thought to sink in.

"But as far as you know your dad never saw a counselor, psychologist, psychiatrist?"

"Not as far as I know."

I jotted a few notes and continued. "Was there anyone on either side of the family who had any difficulty with alcohol?"

She looked at me, "As a matter of fact, my grandfather, my father's father, was alcoholic and he died when I was a little girl."

"Of complications of his alcoholism?"

"Yes, I think so — I don't really remember him very well."

"Anyone else?"

"Hmm." She smiled again. "I can't believe that I was thinking there was nothing going on with my family and it seems to be falling together like this. Actually, I remember now hearing that my dad's younger brother may have had some problem with alcohol at one time, but I don't think he is drinking any more." She hesitated, "But why are you asking about alcohol?"

"Sometimes, even though someone is not treated for depression, use of alcohol is a tip off that there might be some underlying problem that's driving the drink. I'm not trying to say that every alcoholic drinks for that reason, but I believe there are a fair number of people who may."

"It's sort of an attempt to self-medicate?"

"I think so, at least some of the time."

Lisa was thoughtful for a few moments and I said nothing. She then asked, "Wouldn't almost every family include some individuals who had some mood problems or some individuals who drank in a problematic way?"

"Not necessarily. There are some families that seem to have none, or at most have very few of these sorts of issues. During those two years in Vermont when I returned to family practice, probably because I was already trained as a psychiatrist, I would almost always ask questions about emotional history even if the patient had a medical complaint that was unrelated. I was less likely to find a significant family history of mood difficulty if that

was the case compared to the person who came in
with a complaint related to anxiety or depression. I
would also say that when someone came in with a
specific medical complaint that was not mental
health related, but I intuitively felt that the individual may have been dealing with depression, very
often their family history proved to be positive."

"But aren't you really just describing your
impressions? That doesn't sound very much like a
scientific study."

"You're absolutely right. Maybe I didn't ask
questions about mental health with my family practice patient the same way I do with my psychiatric
patients. I certainly might have been prejudiced by
my desire to find what I did, but at least it's an
impression."

"So it's possible that someone who comes in
saying they're depressed might have a family that
seems to be without depression."

"It's possible, but in my experience it's really
rare; that much I can say. And remember, much
about inheritance is not absolute, not a rubber
stamp or a cookie cutter. This is especially true in
mental health. Here we inherit tendencies, vulnerabilities, nuance. The expression of these tendencies
is very often influenced by life experience and environment. But boiling it down, most medical problems of any persuasion do tend to run in families;

and as you are well aware by this point, I truly believe that the difficulties I address as a psychiatrist are just as medical, just as inherited as other health problems that I treated when I was a family doctor.

"So each of us has inherited a body with different internal drug manufacturing capabilities and different staffs of internal physicians."

"And different brain structure and wiring. We really have no control over this body we were given. And...." I paused for emphasis, "It is not a cliche to say that no one is dealt exactly the same deck, except perhaps identical twins. And because of the influence of environment on the expression of the inheritance of identical twins, I believe there are no two people who are exactly alike in this world. The challenge for each of us is to understand the idiosyncrasies of the particular body we have inherited, and to learn how to take care of that body as best we can."

"Interesting." (She obviously loved that word.) Lisa's pretty face scrunched slightly as if she were trying to remember something, "I was listening to a report on the Human Genome Project, and I think someone said that more than ninety-nine percent of all human genes in different people are the same."

"I think I heard the same thing."

"So our genetic differences occur in less than one percent of our genes."

"Sounds like it, but remember it only takes a single amino acid in a genetic code to have a major impact on someone's life."

"Little things mean a lot." She smiled brightly. "No question — genetic mapping will have profound implications for health, both in developing treatments which are non-genetic, and in some cases correcting the genetic problem."

"So some day you'll be able to give me a shot, and voilá! No moodiness."

"Mood regulation, temperament, personality — our humanness, all are so complex that it's difficult to imagine precision tuning. And even though I do prescribe medications to help, I struggle with what is best."

"Why?"

"It's sort of what you said before; part of the beauty of life has to do with contrasts. When someone is anguished and absolutely can't function, and has a plan for suicide, I'll jump in with both feet and insist on medication, hospitalization, or whatever else might be beneficial. But with someone like yourself, the decision of what to do may be more philosophical."

"You mean like whether to use medication?"

"Yep." We were both suddenly quiet. After what seemed like a very long time, but was probably only thirty seconds I said, "Should I go on?"

She looked at me for a second, smiled and said, "No." An appropriate answer to a rhetorical question. Then we both laughed.

·· 7 ··

AFFECTIVE BANDWIDTH

Our moment of levity left good feeling. I asked, "Lisa, why do you think most people come to see me?"

"Because they're depressed?"

"Absolutely right, but let me be more specific. With the possible exception of someone who may be in the midst of a manic or near manic episode, no one comes to me and says, 'Doc, I'm feeling too good and I just don't think I can go on'." She smiled. "The inherited characteristic that ultimately defines which individuals are more likely to seek the help of a psychiatrist is usually not just about the downside we call depression; it has to do with affective bandwidth or emotional range. Feeling great — not manic but just fine, wonderful, productive, happy, creative, energetic, gregarious, exuberant, passionate, all of those things — is what I affectionately call 'affectively enriched'. That's the upside of your emotional bandwidth."

"I'm not sure I understand."

"Well, you came to see me because you were feeling a little down."

"That's right."

"And as you just said, with varying intensity that's probably the main complaint with almost everyone I see."

"Okay."

"From time to time, Lisa, you have experienced a moderate problem with mood that has been an intermittent part of the background noise of your life."

"I think that's right."

"Yet you weren't comfortable enough to see someone had it not been for our chance meeting on the beach."

"Actually, it wasn't chance; I was exercising and saw you leave to go out for your run that morning and I had been thinking about talking to you. But your point is well taken. Anyway, what is this affective bandwidth?"

"You could call it your inherited mood range. You've already mentioned that you have times when you're feeling terrific, so you probably have that wider emotional range or bandwidth than someone whom we'll describe as even-tempered, someone whose mood range always stays in that middle equilibrium area."

"I see what you're driving at. I do have 'up times' as I call them."

"That's good, and it's actually important to me in trying to help you. But for now let's focus on the way you've been feeling recently — somewhat down."

"Okay."

"You are not suffering from a paralyzing depression. I doubt you ever have, although you may tell me I'm wrong about that."

"No, I think that's accurate."

"So right now you're running on half a tank."

"Uh hmm."

"You're dissonant but not devastated; still able to smile and laugh."

"Dissonant really fits."

I continued, "You manage to take care of business but without your usual enthusiasm. You have less passion and little of the joie de vivre than you have at other times, but you're certainly not suicidal."

Lisa nodded.

"You're able to get out of bed and do the things you have to do, and you're not entirely without hope, but you're blah."

"It's like you said before — I have a more moderate depression."

"Exactly."

"Do most people like me usually seek help?"

"I don't think so. I believe that a very large number of people who have the more moderate type of moodiness have no thought of seeking help either because their dissonance is camouflaged by the background noise of day to day comings and goings, and they simply accept it as the way things are; or if they do wonder about their moods, they don't come in because they are uncomfortable with the notion of seeking professional help." She nodded. I waited a moment. "Or, some people might feel that they would somehow be different or lose the essence of themselves if they got treatment. They feel as though there is a hard to define personal value embedded in the angst. It's kind of what you suggested before."

"All of that fits me. I think my moods were sort of camouflaged for awhile; and obviously I did feel uncomfortable with the notion of professional help. But I also was...no, I still am a little afraid of losing myself, especially if I take medication."

"By the time you leave I hope you understand that I believe that doesn't happen. But you must feel truly comfortable about whatever you decide to do, and no matter what that decision is, I will respect it."

"I appreciate that."

"Good." I paused again but there was no further comment from Lisa. "Getting back to what I

said before, the greatest misunderstanding through
the early years of my practice was my lack of appre-
ciation of this notion of affective bandwidth. I
would focus on the downside, everybody's complaint, and generally ignore the upside unless it was
extreme. Psychiatry has taken relatively little notice
of affective enrichment until it reaches a level that is
troublesome, and then the descriptive terms tend to
have a pejorative cast like hypomanic or manic or
high. Your aunt, the one who is manic-depressive,
undoubtedly has a more extreme bandwidth. Her
emotional waves are more like the waves on the
north shore of Hawaii."

"I guess that's right."

"And your grandfather, the toy maker....
Sounds as if he sort of lived enriched most of the
time."

"Hmm. Maybe. That's interesting."

"Having said that, it's important also to remember that emotional inheritance is not passed from
one family member to another in exact form. There
may be obvious similarities between parent and
child, or among various family members; but as I
said, no two people are exactly alike."

"You've got that right."

I smiled. "So, for the sake of discussion, let's say
that about fifty percent of the world's population is
even-tempered. That's not a precise figure, just an

estimate, but I think it's in the ballpark."

"Okay."

"So the other fifty percent or so have inherited an emotional Bandwidth that extends out of that middle equilibrium."

"Does everybody with the wider bandwidth have both the upside and downside?"

"Good question. I don't think so. Some people unfortunately are lopsided down. A few lucky people are lopsided up; as I said, maybe that was your grandfather."

"I sort of remember him that way, but I was really so young...."

"Well, whether or not that was him, it's my impression that most people who are not in that middle even-tempered zone do experience both sides, the depression and the enrichment. Since we met on the beach, let's go back to the ocean metaphor. When you're enriched, you are dancing on the waves or surfing; when you are more or less in the even-tempered zone you're swimming comfortably; and when you've been a bit down as you've been recently, you're treading water. And when someone is more intensely depressed, they may in fact be drowning."

She nodded.

"So imagine what it might be like if most of your time was spent dancing on the waves —

happy, raring to go, filled with energy, thoughts clear, wanting to be with people, attracting people, going through problems like a hot knife through butter."

"It would be terrific."

"And you've been there at times?"

"Not in the extreme, but I've definitely been there."

"Good point. Your enrichment probably doesn't come close to the intensity that occurs with your aunt. But it certainly includes that joie de vivre which has been lacking lately."

"You're right." She suddenly glanced at her watch. "Oh my; I'm sorry, I didn't realize it was so late."

"I thought Ben was at home with David and you were okay with time."

"He is and I'm fine, but I don't want to impose on you."

"I appreciate that, but there's no problem. It's important to me that you at least know where I'm coming from when you think about your options."

"One of which is taking medication?"

"Yes."

·· 8 ··

MEDICATION

1   "There's no requirement that you take medication. I'm certain that you would continue to carry on if you don't take an antidepressant."

    "But what do you think I should do?"

5   "Medication might lead to an improvement in the quality of your life, to a greater consistency of those times when you're feeling well rather than just okay or blah."

    "Hmm."

10   "It's your call, and there's no pressure to decide right now."

    "Okay."

    "But you're hesitant."

    "A little."

15   "So tell me your concerns."

    "Two things. The first is that fear about medication changing or controlling me in some way."

    "Okay."

    "And I'm almost embarrassed to tell you this,

but I'm a little afraid that if I take medication, Ben will regard me as weak or he'll somehow look at me differently." She paused, "I know that probably doesn't make sense because he's encouraged me to see you. Maybe it's just my own fear that I'm dealing with."

"Well, maybe Ben will feel as though this is somehow a reflection of weakness, but I doubt it." I hesitated, "If you would like, even before you decide what to do, I'd be happy to have Ben come in with you so we can all talk."

"Maybe. I'd like to think about that."

"Let me know."

"I will."

"Now about your first concern, whether you'd be changed or controlled in some way?"

"Yes."

"Once someone takes a medication that he or she believes is helpful, I always ask two questions."

"Which are?"

"First, 'Do you feel normal?' As far as I'm concerned, your response to that question has to be yes. You should feel comfortable, not altered or drugged in any way. If you feel drugged or altered or have any significant side effects with any medication I prescribe, I would want you to try something else."

"I have a friend who takes an antidepressant. I forget what it is, but she tells me that it helps because she is less upset about things; yet she feels emotionally numb. I don't want to feel that way."

"That's exactly what I mean. Feeling numb is not normal. I'd probably try to find some other medication that fit her individual chemistry better."

"So how do you know when you have chosen the best medication?"

"A million dollar question. When you begin taking the medication you don't know. It doesn't matter what 'the book' says should happen when you take a particular medication; it's what you say actually does happen that counts. You're the expert. It comes down to your gut feeling, observation, and clear communication between the two of us. My job is to listen carefully."

"So if I say I'm feeling better, what will that tell you?"

"If you say you're feeling better, that's good; but it still may not be clear whether your reaction to that medicine is a bull's-eye or an eighty percent solution."

"So how do you figure out when to keep a medication or try something else?"

"We talk. Sometimes it's not clear whether we have the best fit possible between the medication and your system, but the more we talk the more we're likely to get things right."

"So I could feel somewhat better and relatively

normal and still not have the best possible result?"

"Unfortunately that's true."

"Hmm." She was quiet for a moment and then said, "You mentioned a second question."

"Yes. If you think a medication is working well, I always ask whether there have been moments in your life when you felt just as good without any medication. Perhaps these natural good moments lasted only a few hours or a few days, perhaps it was a long time ago, but no matter when it was or how brief it was you felt good, exactly like you have been feeling since you've begun the medication."

"And most people say they have felt that way before?"

"Yes. I'd say at least ninety-five percent of the time when we're on the right track, people say they feel just the same as they have at those times in the past when they've been at their best. That's the key point. The difference with taking medication is not one of unfamiliar or altered emotional experience; it's one of improved emotional consistency. Without some chemical blending that allows our mood machinery to maintain its efficiency, some of us won't maintain a very comfortable affective state for long periods of time. We tend to slip. It seems to me that the correct chemical blending — finding that fit between the medication or herbs or supplements or foods that we take, and our own internal brain drugs allows an otherwise finicky system to perform optimally in a more consistent way. So the feeling that you have with an ideal response to medication should actually be very familiar."

"Not a false high?"

"Right. As I said, it doesn't make you high, at least not in the way I think you mean. I believe you're thinking of situations in which a substance distorts the perceptions you normally have in your day-to-day life. To me, that's getting high. In other words, it's like drinking seven margaritas, or smoking marijuana; it's not a consciousness you can routinely achieve like the natural mood states we're talking about. My experience has been that medications or nutraceuticals do not create distortions when they are appropriate for your system. If you somehow feel unnatural when you're taking a particular medication or supplement, I would advise you to stop. That may be arbitrary, but I think it's reasonable."

"Sounds reasonable to me."

"Think of running. No matter how hard you might train, no matter how refined your exercise, nutrition and attitude, each of us can only run as fast as the machine we were born with will allow. At our best some of us run faster, some slower. Our running talent is passed to us by our parents who don't have any particular control over the process themselves. I think that our mood talent is passed to us in the same way; therefore, things that help us reach our own mood potential — things such as therapy, exercise, nutritional supplements, a change in diet, acupuncture, meditation, medication - whatever — all have the potential to impact our chemistry and move us towards optimal mood performance. And just like running talent, I believe the optimal mood, which each of us might achieve by efforts to be at our best, is largely defined by that inherited mood talent."

"I understand what you are saying, but I still have a concern."

"Which is?"

"I don't want medication to turn me into a robot?"

"A robot?"

"I have some good days and some days which are not so good. If I were to take medication and feel the same day after day, even if it were always good, I'm not sure that would feel normal."

"Don't worry. If we get the medication right you won't be a robot; but you may feel better a greater portion of the time. If you do have a down day on medication, it may not be as intense as you might have felt without the medication."

"Okay." She smiled, "So, I'll ask you again; do you think I should try medication?"

I smiled back. "That seems reasonable to me, but...."

"I knew there'd be a but."

"But — I'd certainly be willing to suggest a trial of herbs or other supplements first if you felt more comfortable."

"The truth is I've already tried St. John's Wort and Kava Kava, and I didn't notice much change."

"Did you try them together?"

"No, I think that I tried the Kava Kava for a short time and then took the St. John's Wort for a number of weeks."

"Well, Lisa, it's up to you. What is most important is deciding whether you'd really like to engage in this process of adjustment, this journey of self-discovery. And no matter what we try, no decision is set in stone. You're never making any forced long term commitment to take any specific medication, vitamin, or herb; and you certainly would not continue taking something unless you decided it was beneficial." Lisa was nodding.

"By the way, Kava Kava has caused some problems and I think it may have been taken off the market."

"Really?"

"Yes."

"Just because something is not a medication does not mean that it's free from problems. Any chemical can cause a difficulty - an allergic reaction or whatever."

"I didn't have any problems with it."

"Well, that's what I mean by idiosyncrasy; we're all different. If you take any chemical that I prescribe and you think that you're having a side effect, I want you to stop that medication immediately. Don't call me first — stop the medication and then call me to let me know. But more than that, if you try something and you don't have a side effect, but you have even an intuitive sense that the medication or whatever is not right for you, even if you can't articulate why you feel that way, that's okay. It's your call. I'll never be upset if you stop because of your intuition."

"I've read that it takes a while for these medications to work."

"That's often true, but, again, the key word is idiosyncrasy. Whether the medication works at all, how fast it works, what side effects you may have — it's all idiosyncratic. We have a pretty good idea in the abstract of what is supposed to happen when you take a particular medication or herb, but once it's in your unique system with your unique mixture of internal drugs, all bets are off. The key is communication between you and me, and my willingness to trust your instinct about the way that you feel. As far as the time it takes for something to work, if the implication of your question is that it would be possible that we would prematurely stop a medication that might ultimately work, you're absolutely right. What I am suggesting in terms of stopping the medication quickly is not necessarily what all doctors would tell you to do. I am certain that there are times when continuing the medication that initially did not feel right would turn out to have been the right thing. It's just that over the years it has been my experience that intuition about a medication, whether that intuition suggests the medication was good or not good, was ultimately more often correct than incorrect."

"So this is sort of trial and error."

"In a way, but trial and error that is educated and depends on a real collaborative effort."

"You won't have to worry about me communicating with you." She smiled.

"Good."

Then she hesitated, "I know what I want to do; I'd like to try something, but I want to keep my options open. I have to admit that I'm still concerned about Ben's reaction. But I've decided to ask him to come with me next time."

"Good."

"In the meantime, could you give me a prescription for something and let me take it home and think about it?"

··9··

TO TAKE OR NOT TO TAKE?
(THAT IS THE QUESTION)

"Rather than a prescription, I'd be happy to give you samples."

"That sounds good."

"Before we decide what to try.... I remember you mentioned your aunt, the one who's bipolar."

"Yes?"

"Does she take medication?"

"You know, I'm not sure. I assume she does."

"Why don't you get in touch with her and then give me a call."

"So you don't want to just guess."

"Even if we know what helps your aunt, it's still a guess, but it's more educated because you're genetically related and your mood chemistry may be somewhat similar. Are you uncomfortable about speaking with her?"

"Well....Oh, it's silly. I'm a little embarrassed but what the hell," she paused. "I will get in touch with her."

"Good."

Lisa slightly shifted her position and reached for her small purse that was lying on the sofa beside her. I said, "Before you leave, let's go over a few things."

"Okay."

"First of all, are you very sensitive to medications?"

"What do you mean?"

"I mean when you take a medication, do you find that you are affected by a very small dose or do you usually take an amount that would knock out a horse?"

"I'm sensitive. If I take a small amount of an antihistamine, I'm asleep almost immediately. Sometimes taking just one Tylenol gets rid of a headache."

"That's helpful. I usually prescribe starting doses that are low, but with you I'll really go tiny. I don't want someone to reject a medication because of a reaction that wouldn't have happened if the starting dose had been lower."

"Will the dose be enough?"

"Probably not at first; but if you don't have side effects, we can build the dose gradually."

"That makes sense." Lisa hesitated, "If it weren't for my aunt, how would you know which medication to give me? I suppose there's no blood "test to tell you?"

"Not at this point, but there are some basic principles I follow."

"Such as?"

"Without a sort of genetic clue, I make a choice based upon the typical expectations for a given medication. For instance, certain medications are expected to be a little better with anxiety while others may tend to be better with worry and others help with insomnia and so forth. But in every case, even with these expectations, the action of a particular medication in someone's unique system is unpredictable. A medication that statistically is supposed to help with obsessiveness or worry can be dramatically effective with one person and not another. Conversely, a medication which is not expected to be good with obsessive worry may be unpredictably fabulous."

"Really?"

"Yes. And more confusing, even the secondary effects can be very different."

"What do you mean?"

"One person might take a medication and say it's very helpful, but they tend to feel sleepy; another person also feels helped by the same medication, but feels stimulated."

"Can an antidepressant make you worse?"

"Most of the time antidepressants either help or

don't seem to do very much. But occasionally there can be a worsening of symptoms, as though the chemistry that was out of balance becomes a bit more discombobulated."

"So what do you do?"

"You stop the medication. As I said, you have a carte blanche to discontinue anything I prescribe if you think it's not good."

"So we sort of feel our way."

"Right." I hesitated, "But to make things even more interesting, suppose there's some other medical problem that we're not aware of?"

"What do you mean?"

"It's that symphony; one system affects the other. For example, if your thyroid is off kilter, or you have diabetes and your sugar is not well regulated, or you have strong hormonal swings during a menstrual cycle, your mood system could be impacted and knocked a little more out of balance. If that's the case, it may become frustratingly difficult to help your depression until that other system is also recalibrated."

"That's interesting. There are definitely months when I am more irritable premenstrually, and what you just said really makes sense. In fact, during these past weeks it's as though I've had continual PMS."

"Exactly."

Lisa hesitated for a second. "Can you check some of my hormones or other chemicals?"

"I'm glad you mentioned that. Even subtle hormone imbalance can exacerbate depression, and vice versa."

"My mother went through menopause early, in her mid forties, and I've wondered whether I could be perimenopausal. It's subtle, but maybe that's the reason I've felt worse than usual."

"I can't tell you how many women have said exactly the same thing to me. Then they go to their gynecologist only to be told they're not perimenopausal because their lab tests don't show it. I don't think that's right. I'm convinced that some women who are mood vulnerable experience subtle mood changes preceding the changes in their lab tests. Menopause is a multi-year process and the onset can be very subtle but still significant, especially if you're 'depressionally' sensitive. You're thirty-six?"

"Just turned thirty-seven."

"You may be in early perimenopause, especially if your mom was menopausal in her mid forties."

"What should I do?"

"Hormone testing can be tricky, but there are some new techniques that we can use."

"Okay."

"And depending on what shows up, I will probably want to talk with your gynecologist."

"I'm due for a checkup in a month anyway."

"Good. And we'll check a number of other routine labs in order to make sure we're at least not missing a detectable medical problem which could influence your depression or your response to medication."

"That sounds fine."

"To make things even more interesting, Lisa, suppose all of your other body chemistry is just fine, yet a medication doesn't seem to work as you might expect. You have a feeling that something is not breaking through. That may be because of psychological stress."

"What do you mean?"

"Well, your mood chemistry can be altered by internal chemical stress, but also by the stress of losing a job or going through a divorce. It can be altered by stress that occurs when you have a lingering problem from your past that acts like a festering psychological boil, continually agitating your sensitive chemistry."

"What an image."

"I'll try to be more aesthetic, but you understand what I mean?"

"I think I do." She hesitated, "That's where some sort of counseling may be helpful?"

"Exactly."

"So it's not just taking a pill."

"It's as I said before, it's not an either/or. There are some situations in which medication seems to provide comprehensive relief. But often it's just a part of the effort to improve the quality of your life and make things better. It really depends on each person's circumstances. Imagine that you have a kind of pilot light with a minimal flame always warming your internal mood system. When you're abused or hurt in some way as a child, or when you lose your job or are going through a difficult divorce, this pilot light — this Bunsen burner flame — is turned up and the system begins to bubble. Even with the benefit of a medication or some other chemical, the kind of perspective building that occurs in therapy may help turn down the flame and settle the system."

"So in a sense therapy is translated into a change in chemistry?"

"There's more to this than we understand, but I believe that's part of what happens. The experience of feeling better may seem ephemeral or abstract, but when you're feeling good your internal chemistry is different than when you're feeling bad. It's like internal blushing, that constant dynamic ebb and flow of our internal chemistry."

"That's fascinating."

"Does it make sense?"

"I think I understand what you mean now by adjusting chemicals. You mean not just the chemicals in drugs, but other things."

"Right"

"So, what about vitamins? I take them. What do you think about that?"

"Are you asking me whether they will help your mood?"

"Yes."

"Theoretically, I don't know why some wouldn't. I think in individual situations they may help. But doing accurate mood research on individual vitamins and minerals is very difficult for a number of reasons. So let's say that I'm in favor of expensive urine."

"Expensive urine?" Lisa laughed.

"Yes. What I mean is that I think it is probably wise to take nutritional supplements in moderation. A lot of people say that we just pee most vitamins away, and that may be true especially with the water-soluble group, but even so I think it's like an insurance policy. Diets vary. Soils have been depleted. We need some of these micronutrients in our nutritional gasoline, and some may be involved as co-factors in the chemical effectiveness of medication or herbs."

"So you're comfortable with my use of supplements?"

"You don't notice any particular problem or apparent side effects?"

"No. None at all."

"Well, some supplements which are more naturally derived may be better, but I'm comfortable with your continuing in moderation. Perhaps when you come in the next time, you could bring me a list of the different things which you take."

"Okay."

I hesitated. Lisa said nothing further. "So, what do you think about all of this?"

She smiled. "As I said, I'd like to try some medication." The smile faded. "I know my concern about Ben is probably silly, but that's how I feel."

"Maybe those feelings are really more yours than Ben's."

"Maybe. I don't know."

"Years ago when I would help someone who had a strep throat or pneumonia, or when I was suturing a laceration, or especially delivering a baby, the results were gratifying. But for me, the pleasure of watching someone's quality of life dramatically improve as their mood system begins to hum is remarkable. I sometimes feel like I'm watching a rose open. So because of the stigma and ambivalence surrounding psychiatry, I try to spend as much time educating as I can. I want to minimize the possibility that someone would avoid or abandon medication or give up on psychiatry because of unrealistic expectations. If you decide to go on this journey, it's not about a particular medication; it's about a quality of life. I think of myself as practicing 'positive biology,' and that might require carefully trying a few different therapeutic modalities, including medications. So, take your time and really think this through."

"You really don't care much about this, do you?" Lisa's face broke into a broad smile.

I wasn't sure if I was blushing. "I'm just so frustrated about the way people misunderstand psychiatry."

She nodded. "But you're not insisting that I take something?"

"No I'm not. For you there's no urgency. If you were significantly distressed or suicidal, I would try to be more persuasive, but that's not your situation. This is really something that you should feel comfortable about."

"Well, I will call my aunt."

·· 10 ··

RATIONALE

1

When Lisa left my office it was nearly ten p.m. It was too late to return a few non-urgent calls and I was too out of steam to take care of the stack of prescription requests that I hadn't gotten to earlier. I would have to take care of that first thing in the morning.

As I went around turning off lights, checking doors and gathering my "stuff," the idea struck. I had been looking for a particular patient to be the protagonist for a book I wanted to write, and Lisa fit. I'll explain....

In 1994, a few years before that first visit with Lisa, *The Cradle Will Fall* was published. I co-authored this book with my patient. She had asked me to help her tell her story so that other mothers and families would be informed about the potential seriousness of postpartum depression and psychosis.

Michele and I met while she was in the hospital recovering from a self-inflicted gunshot wound. To this day she does not remember shooting either herself or her infant son during a severe post-partum psychosis, but that's what happened. The nurses who were in the emergency room that fateful night in 1987 first had to attempt resuscitation on Michele's deceased infant, who had been carried into the emergency department by his anguished father; they then had to help save Michele's life, knowing what she had done.

The nurses were traumatized and I was asked to meet with them to help work through their distress. That conversation with the nurses evoked more response than any other chapter in the book. I tried to convey the power of the mind, and the power of the medical (chemical) non-psychological aspects of mental health. Many of my patients and members of their families who read the book told me that Chapter Twenty-seven had changed their view of mental illness. The idea of writing a book to expand on the perspectives of that chapter grew.

Sitting there that evening, I realized Lisa was an appealing subject because of her many blessings. No one's life is totally without the detritus of at least a few major and many more minor aggravations. I call it the (Saturday Night Live) "Gilda

Radner" principle: 'It's always something.' I didn't
know Lisa well enough yet to note just what her
"Gilda's" were, but for the most part her life
seemed to have fewer logical, psychological, or
physiological hurdles than most. She had consid-
erable financial comfort; a loving family with husband, child, parents and siblings; good health; a
satisfying career, and the gifts of beauty and intelligence. She would have fewer "reasons" for her
depression, and the genetic, chemical, physiologic,
biologic foundation for her mood changes would
be less confounded by the complexity of life's exi-
gencies.

A second reason that Lisa made a good subject
was the type of depression she had, i.e., relatively
mild! Much literature about depression speaks
mainly to individuals who suffer enormously with
their mood problems, who experience anguish,
who can't get out of bed and can't function, and
who obsessively think of suicide. Although "When
I Became A Psychiatrist..." would speak to anyone
who has experienced depression of any intensity,
its focus would really be a large group of people
like Lisa, who (perhaps appropriately) receive less
attention because their depression is not so bad
and is often camouflaged as part of their "normal
landscape." Like Lisa, this very large group of
modestly depressed individuals go on with their

lives no matter what, are not suicidal, but may at times feel as though they are walking through molasses. I wanted to pay my respects to this group, which I have come to realize includes so many of us.

PART II

TELEPHONE CALLS

·· 11 ··

A FEW DAYS LATER

Idialed and the phone began to ring. I heard the
pickup and Lisa's voice. "Hello."

"Lisa?"

"Hey Carl, thanks for returning my call."

"I hope it's not too late."

"Not at all, we tend to be night owls." There
was a slight pause. "I called to let you know that I
spoke to my aunt, and it turns out she's taking two
medications, an antidepressant called Normac
which she says has helped her enormously, and
another medication called Topakote. I would like to
try it."

"The Normac?"

"Yes."

"I think that's reasonable."

She hesitated slightly. "I also wanted you to
know that I spoke to Ben and he is interested in
joining me. In fact, I was surprised at his response."

"How so?"

"I don't know. I can't explain. But he asked me about our meeting and about your ideas. I tried to explain as best I could."

"So he approves?"

"Of my trying the medication?"

"Yes."

There was a moment of silence at the other end of the line. "He doesn't know." I waited for further comment but there was none.

"When is your appointment?"

"I had scheduled it for the 10th but that's another reason why I'm calling. Ben has to be out of town that day. Could we possibly re-schedule?"

"Sure, I'm going to put you on hold for a minute."

"Okay."

I went to the reception desk and opened my appointment book, penciling a line through Lisa's name on the 10th. I pressed the line button and picked up the phone at the front desk. "You there?"

"Yep."

"I'm looking at my appointment book for a possible time. What about Tuesday the 17th at 7:30?"

"A week later; that sounds good. I'll check with Ben and if there's a problem I'll call, otherwise we'll be there." She hesitated, "I was reading information about these medications?" She left the question hanging.

"Yes?"

"It says that it might take three to six weeks to work."

"That may be true."

"Well, you told me that if I felt that the medication was not right for me, I could stop it right away. If I do that based on my hunch, how do I know that it wouldn't have worked if we waited?"

"Actually, we wouldn't know. As I mentioned, we could be wrong. But I've watched many people persevere despite those negative intuitions, and more often than not that initial impression proved to be correct."

"Really?"

"Yes. But it's not always true. As we discussed, sometimes the medication would have eventually worked."

"But you think intuition is more often correct?"

"Yes." I hesitated for a moment. "Lisa, besides the side effects that cause a small percentage of people to stop any particular medication, there are really three early responses someone might have. Most of the time, especially at low doses, nothing seems to happen. And that's good. In that instance we gradually increase the dose; eventually you will get a sense of the medication, but it may take a few weeks."

"Okay."

"Second, you may have a positive feeling which may be subtle or obvious, but at least there is something hopeful from the beginning."

"Okay."

"And third is the scenario we've been discussing, where you don't like the medication for some reason that you may not even be able to explain."

"And we stop even though we may be stopping a medication that might eventually work?"

"That's right, the call is really yours. You are the only person who knows exactly how you feel. If your intuition tells you to stop the medication, we stop. But remember, no decision about taking or not taking medication is carved in stone. Responding to evolving circumstance is part of the journey. If we stop something early and it turns out that a few other medications don't pan out, nothing prevents us from going back to that first medication that we had stopped very quickly — and trying again."

"I guess that's true." I waited. Lisa said nothing more.

"I'll give you some Normac samples. If you have any problems or questions, call me. Otherwise I'll see you and Ben on the 17th."

"OK." She hesitated, "Could I ask you one more question?"

"Sure."

"Should someone who is taking medication also be in counseling?"

"Is this you specifically, or are we talking in the abstract?"

"Both."

"Well, there's not exactly an either/or answer. Counseling is not necessarily just an activity to deal with problems, it also has the capacity to expand one's vision or horizons; in some sense, everyone who lives experiences counseling with family members and friends. Probably every civilization has had its guides of one sort or another, and there are undoubtedly some people who would not benefit from medication, but would benefit from therapy with the right individual."

"So, what about me?"

"First of all, if you're taking medication, we have to meet from time to time anyway, and I would use those opportunities for more than simply asking you about problems with medication. There is an art to using medication for mood problems and I don't like to trivialize "medication management". I always want to talk in some depth and especially want everyone to understand and feel comfortable about what we're doing. So, in a sense, we're inevitably going to be doing some counseling."

Lisa nodded, "I appreciate that, but I guess

I'm asking more about the need to come in for regular therapy in addition."

"As far as you're concerned, Lisa, if you felt the need to come in and talk about something, now or at any time, I would encourage that. If I thought there was something that you should be dealing with, even though you might seem disinterested in therapy, I would tell you."

"So, do you feel I'm in that position? Should I come in weekly?"

"So far, in that narrow perspective, I don't really think so."

"That's good."

"Maybe it's good, or maybe I'm just missing the boat."

"I don't think you are."

"That's good."

"That was my line."

I chuckled.

She continued, "So, how would you answer the question about counseling in the abstract if we weren't talking about me?"

"If I had any sense that there was a possibility of benefit, of if things were not going well with just medication, I am almost always inclined to suggest counseling along with medication. That is definitely preferable. But let's deal with an unrealistic hypothetical to make things clearer. Suppose you came to me and said the emperor had granted you permission to seek my help, but I was only permitted either to prescribe medication or engage you in counseling. I wasn't allowed to do both. Presented with that dilemma, most of the time I would probably write a prescription."

"Because of the chemical imbalance?"

"Yes. Ironically, in some instances straightening out your chemistry with the use of medication seems to relieve some of the apparent need for therapy."

"You mean it changes the way you think about things?"

"Let's say there's a shift in perspective. That may be difficult to accept, but I believe it's true. I think it was John Milton who said, 'The mind is its own place, and in itself, can make a heaven of hell, a hell of heaven.' So much of life is perception, and so much perception is as much between the ears as what is out there. Sometimes mountains shrink to molehills when your chemistry is optimal."

"I understand, and I agree, but it bothers me a little to think that we are so..,." she thought for a moment, "so perceptually fragile."

I smiled. "I know exactly what you mean, yet I've seen many people who've felt intensely about something, then begin to see things differently when they respond to medication. But don't get me wrong, I've also seen a lot of people who've responded well to medication who continue to have a need to talk about certain issues in their life. And ironically, when that happens, when they're feeling better with medication, in a sense they're better at therapy."

"What do you mean better?"

"More effective. More able to face their issues."

"Makes sense."

"It especially makes sense now that we understand that the adult brain is able to physically change in ways that will either improve mood or make mood regulation worse."

"You mean the brain grows after childhood?"

"Probably, but also the connection between cells seems to become more complicated and robust as though fertilizer has been applied, or more sparse as though there has been a pruning process; so our emotional circuits may become 'smarter' or 'dumber'."

"Really?"

"Nah." I laughed. Then I quickly said – "All joking aside, we think that might be what's happening."

Lisa smiled, "So what makes mood circuits become smarter?"

"Learning new concepts for one thing. When we learn, wiring actually changes. I think it's possible that talk therapy stimulates intelligent self-learning and therefore may actually lead to some rewiring."

"Really?"

"Um huh."

Lisa smiled, "But I guess you'd have to keep talking."

"I don't think anyone knows the dosing of talk therapy, but I suspect that once you had 'learned' a new way of looking at your life, those changes might be sustained – perhaps with an occasional learning booster – like returning briefly to therapy or reading an appropriate book, or having an appropriate conversation with a good friend."

"What else might enhance the wiring?"

"Probably chemicals – perhaps fish oil – possibly antidepressants; we're just learning about this. Now I'm just guessing about the fish oil, because I've not actually read any specific research relating the oil to neurogenesis, but there is an old saw about eating more fish to become smarter. And there is some evidence to suggest that higher dietary intake of fish leads to improved mood stability."

"Did you say that antidepressants might enhance wiring as well?"

"It's possible that some of the effectiveness of antidepressants may reflect stimulation of new brain branching."

"Above and beyond the chemical regulation?"

"Yes."

"This is fascinating."

"Food for thought."

She was silent and I could imagine that she was smiling.

"But having said all of that, as far as medication is concerned, I have to tell you we do have a emperor who does push for more pills and less counseling."

"What do you mean you have an emperor?"

"It's really emperors – insurance companies. Because insurers perceive that medication is the core treatment and counseling is additional and ongoing treatment, which adds too much cost, they limit the amount of counseling they will pay for."

"Really?"

"Really, but don't get me started. Anyway, I'll leave some samples for you at the front desk. After a week or so give me a call, but call sooner with any problem."

"OK."

"And when you bring Ben, ask me again about counseling."

"Why?"

"Because of our ability to look inside the brain and see changes with counseling, but I'll explain later."

Rash Decisions

About ten days later, Lisa called again. By the time I responded to the message it was almost 10:00 p.m.

"Running late?" I could tell that she was smiling.

"That's me."

"Well thanks for calling back. I wanted to tell you that I started the Normac and it seemed to be working."

"Good."

"Not really."

"Why?"

"Because I don't think I can take it."

"Why not?"

"I developed a slight rash on my chest and back. I didn't think much of it at first, but after a day or two it dawned on me that it might be from the medication, so I did what you said."

"What do you mean?"

"I stopped the medication. That was three or four days ago." She hesitated.

"Any change with the rash?"

"It's gone."

"How do you feel?"

"You mean mood wise?"

"Yes."

"A little aggravated, actually. The change I thought I was feeling was so subtle, it's hard to say now — but I did think I was beginning to feel better and I was a little excited that this would really be helpful. I guess I can't continue it. Right?"

"We can't be one hundred percent sure that the rash was related to the Normac, but it's possible. We could restart it to make sure, but it's probably better that you've stopped."

"That's disappointing."

"I know, but we have many options, many other antidepressants. The good news — if you were responding to the Normac, it tends to confirm that there is some internal chemistry that is out of balance."

"Why do you say that?"

"Do you remember when I spoke about the fifty percent or so of people who are even-tempered?"

"Yes."

"I think that group does not respond much to any antidepressant because they have no significant chemical imbalance to address."

"Hmm." There was a thoughtful pause, "So antidepressants are not just stimulants."

"That's right. They're not stimulants and they're not tranquilizers. For instance, a tranquilizer is likely to affect almost all people in a predictable way. Did I explain that before?"

"You may have, but explain it again."

"The point is, even if someone is not particularly nervous, enough Valium or Xanax or Ativan or whatever will usually cause a sort of mellowing. Given a sufficient dose, the effects can be felt even if someone is not particularly anxious to begin with. In contrast, not all people will react to an antidepressant."

"But anyone could develop a rash from an antidepressant?"

"Absolutely. You can have an allergic reaction to almost anything that you put into your system, whether it's Normac, Valium, or strawberries."

For a few moments there was silence on the other end of the line. "So I guess, as you said, I'll never know for sure if Normac would have helped."

"That's probably true. But if we get stuck and nothing we try seems to work, we might cautiously re-try. Maybe it didn't cause the rash; we just don't know."

"But for now we try something else."

"I think that's best."

"So what should I try?"

"Come by and I'll leave samples of Happox with Dawn."

"Okay."

"They're ten milligram tablets and that's the smallest dose available. Unfortunately, they are not scored, but it's okay to break them. Why don't you get a pill splitter and try taking a half tablet after your evening meal."

"What's the usual starting dose?"

"Twenty to forty milligrams."

"So five milligrams is really minimal?"

"Yes."

"That's good. And I should call you in a couple of days?"

"Yes. And same instructions. Stop the Happox immediately if you think you're having a significant side effect or allergic reaction. Also stop it at your discretion if you think that it's not the right medication for you."

"Will do."

"And Ben knows?"

There was a hesitation, "Not yet."

·· 13 ··

BINGO

This time when Lisa called, she caught me between patients.

"Hey."

"I can't believe I got you."

"Your timing was perfect."

"Well, I just wanted to say bingo."

"What do you mean?"

"I mean I've been on the Happox for about a week and there is no question in my mind about how I'm feeling. I'm beginning to feel like my old self."

"And still only five milligrams?"

"Still only five. I read the package insert and I know the dose is low and I know I have responded more quickly than is usual, but I told you I've always been extremely sensitive to medication."

"I'm glad you're feeling better."

"Me too."

"So you and Ben are coming in on Tuesday

night?"

"That's the plan."

"And….?"

"Ben doesn't know."

"Lisa…"

"I know."

PART III

LISA & BEN

·· 14 ··

Sugar and Spice and Stainless Steel

Even though Ben and I knew each other pretty well, he seemed slightly nervous; but I didn't pay much attention. This was a difficult situation and a lot of people are uncomfortable the first time in a psychiatrist's office. He smiled and extended his hand. "Good to see you."

"You too."

Lisa said, "Thanks for seeing us so late."

"No problem. Glad we could get together."

The three of us walked from the waiting room to my office. "You really do have a couch." Ben was smiling.

"I know, I sometimes feel like a cliche — the beard, the sofa — but the beard appeared on a camping trip years before I switched to psychiatry, and the sofa is space efficient seating, not Freudian."

"What do you mean 'switched to psychiatry'?"

"Carl was a family doctor before he became a

psychiatrist. There is a whole story that I'll tell you later."

Ben looked at me, "It's interesting that with all the conversations we've had, I never knew that."

"True." I shrugged.

"For that matter you've never really talked about psychiatry."

"It's not a usual locker room subject."

Ben smiled, but in a slightly preoccupied way, "Lisa was explaining some of your ideas."

"Trying to explain." She had an uncomfortable half smile.

"So what did she say?"

"That you think psychiatric problems are medical, not psychological."

"Let's say substantially medical." I hesitated. Every time I tried to explain my perceptions about mental health, they had a slightly different ring, hopefully reflecting what might make sense to the person I was speaking with at the time. "These ideas I have are not gospel, they're more like food for thought."

"Okay."

"Psychology, stress, life experience — whatever you wish to call it is very important, but it's not the whole story."

Ben nodded. "Understood."

"So, as Lisa just mentioned, after I finished my

training in psychiatry I did return to family practice. Lisa can fill you in on the details, but what happened when I made that switch was very interesting. Your son's name is David, is that right?"

"Yes."

"And he's about six?"

"Right. Why do you ask?"

"I was wondering if you and Lisa are going to agree with what I am about to explain. With my return to family practice, I again saw infants and young children for typical pediatric problems and checkups; but now I had the eyes of a psychiatrist. I couldn't help but notice the often dramatic personality differences between siblings — like night and day."

"Why did you think that was so unusual?" Lisa chimed in.

"That's exactly the point, Lisa. I didn't think it was unusual, but it didn't entirely fit with the emphasis of my psychiatry training. Remember, this was about twenty-five years ago and psychiatric education was quite different than it is now. At that time, teaching was focused primarily on dynamic psychology as the primary cause of problems, and even then that never felt entirely correct. As I met these young families in Bennington, with siblings who were strikingly different, I became increasingly convinced that differences in personality and temperament should not be attributed primarily to psychology. Siblings certainly had different birth order, were of different sexes, obviously had different personal experiences — but they likely had an enormous number of shared influences. They lived in the same home, with the same parents, had the same relatives, enjoyed a similar diet, experienced the same socioeconomic status, went to the same schools, had a similar peer pool." Both Bradys were nodding. "I didn't expect siblings to be clones of one another, but with so many psychological, social, and environmental factors shared, wouldn't they at least tend to be alike? And some were, but many weren't."

"Interesting," Ben said. (I was realizing that both Bradys had a fondness for that word.)

"When parents agreed that their children were very different from one another, I would ask, 'When did you first notice that your son was this way or your daughter was that way?' and the answer I got, almost every time, was 'From the day they were born.' Some women even volunteered that their children were different in the womb and that the difference was consistent. 'Susan kicked the hell out of me and Tommy was relatively quiet; and they're still that way.'"

Lisa smiled as if she were remembering David's womb activity.

"Has David been consistent in his personality or temperament?"

Ben and Lisa looked at each other; both turned to me and nodded yes.

"So you feel that he has been 'David' from the day he was born?"

"Absolutely," they spoke in unison.

"Where was Freud that first day?"

The Bradys smiled again.

"Don't get me wrong! Psychology and stress are important and influential, but I believe we all come into this world with our own temperament, our own way of being, our own way to connect with people and our environment. Whatever this is — this essence, this uniqueness we all have — it's as much a physical characteristic as blue eyes or brown, tallness or shortness, muscularity or leanness, quickness or slowness, musicality or tone deafness. We're all different from the beginning, from before we've had any chance to be shaped or caressed or influenced by life."

They both sat silent.

"You guys are like Ronnie and me; we also have one son. So in our situations you can't really compare David or Eli to siblings; but we do feel there has been a consistency about Eli's temperament and personality from the day he was born."

It was Lisa who spoke. "This is the old nature

versus nurture/environment versus heredity question, isn't it?"

"Exactly."

"And you think it's nature or heredity that's
dominant?" It was Ben.

"Yes. Nature and nurture dance the tango of
life together, but nature leads."

"So the psychological impact of a similar experience may be very different from one person to the
next?"

"Maybe I'm wrong, Lisa, but that's what I
think. It's like taking the same picture with different
filters on the camera."

Ben immediately asked, "So what role do parents play in the development of their children?"

"Great question. For the sake of discussion let's
say that you had three children, one who was steel,
one silk, and one gold. And let's say that you wanted them all to be steel. At this point I believe that no
matter how hard you try, as a parent you cannot
make that happen. The differences related to a
child's intrauterine environment, life experience,
psychological bumps, parenting efforts and the like
may determine whether the steel is stainless or rusty,
whether the silk is a beautiful scarf or a tattered rag,
whether the gold is eighteen carat or fourteen carat,
but at this point I strongly believe that the steel stays
steel, the silk stays silk, and the gold remains gold."

"So the steel child has a different temperament chemistry than the silk child?" Ben asked.

"Again, that's what I believe."

"And that's related to the notion that depression involves chemistry?"

"Right, Ben. But the idea that chemical imbalance is required for depression is no different than other medical problems."

"What do you mean?"

"You can't have diabetes without an imbalance in your sugar regulating chemistry. The same could be said for your digestive chemistry and ulcers or your thyroid chemistry and various thyroid problems. That chemical imbalance is the common denominator of many medical problems."

Lisa added, "Even getting a cold may have as much to do with the chemical efficiency of your immune system, more than whether or not you're exposed to a virus. "

I burst out laughing.

Lisa looked slightly chagrined. "Did I say something wrong?"

"Absolutely not, I'm sorry — didn't mean to laugh, but it's sort of a compliment. You are remarkably clear and articulate."

Lisa blushed.

·· 15 ··

THE BLUSH

1 “**B**en, did you notice that?”

“Notice what?”

“That Lisa blushed.”

5 “She always blushes.”

Lisa blushed even more. Ben and I were both smiling.

“Your blush is well-timed.”

“Why?”

10 “Because blushing is a good example of the kind of continuous chemical adjusting that goes on between mind and body. You just blushed and you weren't touched physically. You responded to an emotion, embarrassment, and suddenly your face 15 became red. You dispensed an internally manufac- tured drug that triggered your autonomic nervous system to cause vasodilation. In response to stress or emotion, either positive or negative, a sort of blushing is occurring constantly in organs in our

body. So what we perceive and think has a continuous influence on our body chemistry, and our body chemistry has a continuous influence on what we perceive or think. This can be a happy cycle or a vicious cycle. Seem reasonable?"

Ben nodded, "Um hum."

"Suppose I had a magic camera that could take pictures of your brain chemistry and each of your hundred plus 'mood drugs' was represented by a different color. Suppose also that you and Lisa were both sad when you came into this office and I took 'before' snapshots. Then, as you both were about to leave and were happier, I took 'after' pictures. I'm sure the 'after' colors would look different than the 'before' colors. There are so many factors that can provoke that 'color' change: external stress, current experience, old personal history that festers for years, internal chemical stresses such as a malfunctioning thyroid, hormonal swings of a menstrual cycle, changes in blood sugar, infectious agents — and on and on; mind-body and body-mind!"

Lisa commented, "So this explains why I seem to get a little down when I have a cold?"

"Exactly. And it's also why you seem to get a cold more frequently when you're a little down to begin with. In order for any of us to feel depressed or anxious or excited or confused or happy or sad, something has to change in our brain chemistry.

Think of these chemical changes as internal blushing. When you are depressed, whatever the cause, your mood system is chemically different than when you are happy."

Ben made a "hmm" sound in his throat. "This really makes so much sense."

"I think it does. And what's really remarkable is that most of the time our bodies adjust well and take care of our needs automatically. But when that's not the case, when our chemistry in a certain area is out of whack, that's where doctors and other sorts of healers come in. The challenge for each of us individually is to identify those parts of our personal machinery that are more sensitive and vulnerable. I try not to interfere with this marvelous internal health system that we all have unless it really seems to be necessary. And that certainly includes non-interference in terms of mood regulation. But when your mood system or your blood pressure system or your sugar system needs a little help, I try to help as delicately as I know how." Something at that moment made me glance towards Lisa and our eyes met. I thought she blushed again faintly, which I assumed was related to the fact that she hadn't told Ben she was taking medication. I thought he hadn't noticed, but I wasn't sure.

I quickly continued, "The implication that prescribed medications are intrinsically bad chemicals,

necessary evils, while herbs, vitamins, and foods are
good chemicals has to be re-thought. I try to be as
constrained and judicious as possible where medication is concerned, but I also try to look at the
other chemicals we ingest without accepting that
they are always benign."

"So", Lisa said, "when you prescribe medicine,
or when I take an herb, or change my diet, or when
I'm exercising or going to an acupuncturist, my
chemistry is being adjusted."

"Right — and I'm glad you mentioned exercise.
While I was still in medical school, my father had a
heart attack. Shortly after that I began jogging on a
daily basis. In addition to improving my cardiovascular fitness, exercise causes release of internally
manufactured brain drugs, which tends to create a
better mood. So it's not a medication or something
else proposition. There is no reason just to have
medication, or just to do therapy, or just suggest
exercise or meditation or acupuncture or neuromodulation or whatever. Sometimes one and one
equals three."

"Makes sense."

"But let's talk about therapy for a moment.
Everybody asks."

"Before we talk about therapy, you just mentioned a word that I have never heard."

"Neuromodulation?"

"That's it," Lisa said.

"I threw that in to see if you'd catch it."

"Well, I win." She smiled.

"Me too," Ben said, not to be left out.

"It's an important concept. In the broadest sense, any adjustment of the neuro-environment of the brain might be considered neuromodulation. We've primarily been talking about the neuromodulation provided by the ingestion of chemicals, whether they are called herbs or nutriceuticals or medications or foods. But the word has not really been used much until recently, and it's currently referring more specifically to brain adjustments that are provoked by the application or impact of electromagnetic influence."

"Like shock treatment?"

"Yep. Like ECT."

"ECT is shock treatment?"

"Yes. Electroconvulsive therapy. Much more sophisticated and safer than in the Jack Nicholson "One Flew Over The Cuckoo's Nest." Very, very effective, but not without side effects."

"Makes me shudder." Lisa said. "Aren't there newer treatments that are better?"

"For some people, newer – and maybe even older treatments that are better."

"Older?"

"Well, acupuncture and possibly some treat-

ments attributed to ancient Tibetan cultures really
depend upon electrical or magnetic modulation."

"Really?"

I turned to Ben, "Does she always ask that?"

"Well, she uses that word a lot, but I have never
mentioned it."

"Interesting," Lisa said.

I laughed.

"So you can use these neuromodulation treatments instead of medication?" Ben asked.

"Sometimes instead of, but sometimes in conjunction with medication." I paused, neither Brady
seemed to have anything further to say, and I didn't
want to go off on a neuromodulation tangent.
Finally, I said, "So, we can get back to discussing
therapy?"

"Okay."

"Well – talking with someone in a way that
occurs in therapy concentrates one's focus on life
and that may be a very helpful catalyst in provoking new understanding. Think of your mood regulating system as having a sort of a pilot light that
keeps things percolating. When you're upset or agitated, the flame is turned up."

"You're being neuromodulated?" Lisa asked.

"Exactly. And when that flame gets turned up,
it makes sense that there would be more percolation
and imbalance – or more neuromodulation – in a

sensitive system than in a tougher one. If problems fester from your early childhood, the flame may be continuously turned up. If you lose your job, the flame may be turned up temporarily. In any situation in which you're upset or agitated, the flame is higher. As you come to grips with issues or situations or problems in your life, the pilot may be adjusted down a bit; and a sensitive system, whether it's mood or digestion or sugar, is given a bit of a break. There is less likelihood of the chemical imbalance."

"Is there always some sort of stress which pushes a sensitive system out of balance?"

"No, Ben, but it's another good question. Sometimes a delicate system can simply evolve out of balance without any external or internal provocation. There is a biological rhythm to any body system. Think about any medical problem — ulcers, arthritis, angina, gout – it will vary in intensity — better, worse, better, worse — or it simply comes and goes. No medical problem stays exactly the same all the time. There is continuous ebb and flow. Then, on top of that, if stress hits a vulnerable system during a time of increased vulnerability, it may provoke the system to an imbalanced state."

Both Bradys began to speak at the same moment.

·· 16 ··

BEN

"I'm sorry honey, go ahead."

"No, you first," Ben insisted.

Lisa glanced at me fleetingly and then spoke to Ben. "You know how I tend to become moody at times — maybe a little depressed?"

He looked towards his wife with a curious expression. "Sure. Isn't that why you saw Carl in the first place?"

"Yes, it is. And after my last visit I wanted to try some medication but I felt uneasy because I thought you might not like it."

"Why wouldn't I like it?"

"Well I know it's...." She glanced at the floor and then looked back at Ben, "I wondered if you would think I was weak or something like that?" She smiled.

Ben's eyes suddenly had tears. He tried to blink them back.

"Ben, what is it? " She slid closer to him and put her arm around his shoulders. He didn't speak. The Kleenex was on the arm of the sofa next to him, and Lisa pulled a few tissues and put them into his hand. After a few moments he wiped his eyes, blew his nose and took a deep breath. She removed her arm from him shoulders and slid away a few inches so she could turn and look more directly at him.

"Lisa, I...." He took another big breath. "Lisa, I'm sorry. I feel like a jerk. I'm taking a medication called Happox. I began taking it just before we met, and the thing is — at first I was afraid to tell you, and then, I don't know — it just never seemed to be the right time to talk about it."

"I don't know what to say." Lisa looked at me and I couldn't tell whether she was going to laugh or cry. There was silence. I wasn't sure what to say either. Ben's head was down.

"Damn." Ben reached over and took a few tissues and dabbed his eyes again. "Lisa, I would want you to do whatever would be best for you. In fact, I was glad you were going to see Carl and almost suggested that you try something if he thought it was a good idea. But I didn't say anything because I felt so guilty." He didn't look directly at Lisa, just pursed his lips and shook his head. "And lately..." He suddenly stopped and stared at Lisa, "You are taking medication too? That's why you've seemed better?"

Lisa nodded. Ben again dabbed his eyes and took another deep breath, "Before Lisa and I met, I was involved with someone. We were briefly engaged but I knew it wasn't right, and I called it off. Lisa knows all about that. What I never said was — despite the fact that I instigated that breakup; it was very difficult. I wondered if I was making a mistake. And Barbara, my former fiancée, was very hurt. Anyway, I became depressed. I have a close friend who is a doctor, and he suggested I try Happox. Normally I wouldn't have considered it, but I did — and it helped. I was still taking it when I met Lisa a few months later. I knew from the moment Lisa and I met that she was my soul mate. I didn't want to do anything that would put our relationship at risk. I hadn't thought much about the Happox until then, but suddenly I felt ashamed. I didn't want to tell her about it, but I was reluctant to stop because I felt well and didn't really know how I would feel without it. It was sort of a damned if you do and damned if you don't situation. In my mind at the time, I figured I would either stop or tell her soon enough, but somehow I never did. Actually, when I found out you were a psychiatrist, it stirred my guilt. I was glad when Lisa said that she might see you, but I was apprehensive because I knew it would come up."

"Anything else you haven't told me?" This could have been a heavy question, but Lisa was smiling.

"Nothing. Nothing I can think of. I am truly sorry."

Lisa turned towards me and shook her head. "Isn't this ridiculous? Why should we be so ashamed?"

"I couldn't agree more. You have no idea of the number of people I've seen through the years who were embarrassed or ashamed because of taking antidepressants. Using medication for any medical problem is not to be taken lightly; but with depression, more than with any medical problem I've ever treated, taking medication is considered a sign of weakness. When I would treat hypertension successfully, there was rarely if ever any issue of loss of self-respect or of having a flawed character because medication was used. The goal remained lowering blood pressure. But when I prescribe medication for depression, the picture is often different. This didn't happen with you, Ben, but usually when someone feels better or, as I prefer to think, more normal or optimal as a result of taking antidepressant medication, a bit of alchemy occurs and very quickly the goal is transformed from lowering the anguish to 'getting off the medication.'"

"Why is that?" Ben asked.

"There are still a lot of people who think that seeing a psychiatrist is equivalent to being weak or crazy."

"Don't you think we're getting beyond that?"

"In part..." Lisa interrupted me and answered her own question, "Maybe we're getting a little beyond it, but I have to be honest. Even I felt a little bit that way in my heart of hearts when I was running with you that morning on the beach. I mean, I know better but obviously that stigma was still hanging around. If I'd had a skin problem, I would have gone to a dermatologist immediately. Yet I was troubled for years by moodiness and I resisted seeing a psychiatrist"

"The situation is improving, but it's still not great. And ironically one of the problems is the fact that we are aware of our emotions, but not as aware of the blood pressure or sugar or uric acid measurements that are relevant to other medical problems. Because you are aware of your emotions, it's easy to assume that they should be under your control. When it seems that's not the case, we feel weak. We more easily accept the fact that we cannot completely control blood pressure or blood sugar. It somehow seems reasonable that those medical problems reflect machinery that we've inherited, and therefore blending our nutritional gasoline to help those parts of our machinery is acceptable. It doesn't matter whether we have to adjust diet or take medications or herbs. It's okay with diabetes or hypertension, but not okay with depression. That's weakness."

"So you really think that reducing depression and reducing blood pressure are equivalent situations?"

"Yes, Ben, I really do. Both are medical problems that require a readjustment or rebalancing of body chemistry that is out of whack. Anything that helps to do that is relevant. If your body chemistry improves because you have engaged in physical conditioning, or you've benefitted from therapy, or from meditation, or acupuncture, or you take a medication, that's all great. But — and this is a big but — if you do not persist in continuing the efforts to help your vulnerable body chemistry to operate as efficiently as possible, you're likely to return to whatever health problem you started with."

"So you're saying that we can't really cure many medical problems, we can just make them better as long as we're actively treating them?"

"That's the way I look at it. You can keep the symptoms of a medical problem at bay, but until we are able to treat something by manipulating genes, we can't really eliminate the inherent vulnerability that we are born with."

"Interesting."

I smiled and nodded to Ben; there was that word again. But he definitely seemed more comfortable.

·· 17 ··

Tests

"Can you identify depression with a blood test?"

"Not with a blood test, Ben, but there are some sophisticated brain imaging studies that do show differences between individuals who are depressed and individuals who aren't depressed. There are also computerized EEG techniques, brain wave tests, that demonstrate underlying electrical differences between people who are depressed and not depressed. But all of these studies are expensive, and at this point they usually confirm what we already know clinically."

"That reminds me," Lisa said, "How did my lab work come out?"

"Forgive me. I did get your results and I meant to call you."

"That's okay."

"Everything was fine."

"What were you looking for?" Ben asked.

"I was looking for signs of other medical problems that could impact Lisa's mood system. Remember, mind/body or body/mind medicine is real. If I had identified a thyroid problem, a liver problem, diabetes, low magnesium, anemia and so forth, that would have helped in putting the whole picture together; but Lisa's lab results were absolutely normal.

"Including hormonal levels?"

"Yes."

"That's good," Ben said.

"That's true," I smiled.

But Ben immediately said, "I have another question."

"Which is?"

"There were times when I was younger when maybe I would feel a little down or moody, but certainly nothing like I experienced when I ended my engagement. And that wasn't the first time I'd broken up with a girlfriend or had a stressful situation. So why did I react so strongly then?"

"I really don't know. Other than the obvious, that that situation was particularly upsetting, I can't tell you exactly why then and not before. Maybe you were in the midst of a natural chemical downturn in your mood chemistry during that difficult period and that might explain it. But think of this: if you asked me the same question about why some other medical problem starts at a particular moment in time, some problem that you've never had before, I couldn't answer that either. The person with arthritis had to have a first day. He or she probably never had more than an occasional ache or pain until that first episode. The diabetic has normal blood sugar before that first abnormal test; before someone develops high blood pressure, they have normal blood pressure. Mood problems act just like other medical problems, because they are medical problems! You're born with a certain medical vulnerability. Why that particular vulnerability shows itself at a given moment in someone's life, whether it occurs spontaneously or because of some obvious stress, is something that we don't yet understand."

"Hmm. I really never thought about it that way." Ben hesitated, "I know I'm jumping around, but I've never had a chance to ask questions before."

"Fire away."

IDIOSYNCRASY

"I've been taking Happox for seven years, is there some harm in that? Should I stop?"

"I feel a bit uncomfortable.... Who prescribed your Happox?"

"Dr. Mensh, and I will talk to him, but I'd like to know your thinking on this. In the past he has suggested that I stop and see how I feel, but for some reason I've not done it, and he's never pressed the issue."

"What I have to say is not necessarily what Ron would say. But I'd be happy to talk with him with your permission."

"I understand that you and he may differ, and I would have no objections if you spoke with him."

"Okay. Well, first of all, I always want someone to be a real partner in the decision making process. Let's assume that you wanted to stop the medication to see how you feel after all this time."

"Okay."

"Unless I believe you would be at risk for suicide or some other serious consequence, I probably wouldn't try to persuade you to continue."

"So through the years many patients have decided to stop?" Lisa asked.

"Yes." I hesitated for a moment, "It's important to remember that deciding whether to continue or not continue a medication is not a permanent decision. You're never signing an irrevocable contract; you can always change your mind."

"So why not take the medication just when you need it?"

"You can do that, Lisa, and that may work for some people. One issue that arises, however, is the slowness of the response to these medications that some people experience. You can't take an antidepressant and predict that you'll feel better the next day. It may take a few weeks. If you allow yourself to be exposed to the recurrent depression by stopping, by the time the depression is back under control you may have had a difficult month or two. And there is another very important reason which is not always appreciated."

"What's that?" Ben asked.

"It has to do with what we were talking about a little while ago. Our bodies operate as though we have our own internal tides. These tides ebb and flow in cycles, a few of which are obvious."

"Like the menstrual cycle?" Lisa again.

"Exactly. But because so many of these internal clocks tick silently, our tides are often reflected in subtle ways like variations in energy, alertness, or athletic performance. But we also experience these tides by the unexpected return or worsening of medical problems like ulcers, arthritis, migraines, or depression — even when there is no obvious psychological stress or other cause."

"So medical problems sometimes come and go just because of body rhythms."

"Yes."

"So if someone stops taking medication, you would expect the depression to return at some point. Is that what you're saying?"

"Yes. If you have had depression more than a couple of times in your life, it's likely to return."

"So Ben hasn't hurt himself by taking the medication for seven years?"

"Probably not."

"Probably?"

"There are a lot of 'probablies'. Too often we doctors forget how much we don't know. For instance, I am often handed a list of six or seven medications that someone is taking and asked if the medication I'm about to prescribe is compatible, and I can search in a computer and look in books for drug interactions and find none listed. That is a pretty good review comparing one medication with another, but I can't really compare how one medication will react with the six other medications at the same time. This is especially true in a particular person's body with its own bouillabaisse of internal chemicals. This is what idiosyncrasy is all about. Those seven medications might be just fine for nine hundred ninety-nine out of a thousand people, but one person may have an unexpected reaction of some kind. The same principle might apply to any chemical we ingest, whether we call it a food, an herb, or medication. Some people have side effects to milk; some can't eat wheat. There's a real difference between the chemicals that are intrinsically toxic to virtually anyone and chemicals that are idiosyncratically inappropriate for some people, and very helpful to others."

"So how do you protect yourself from substances that may be harmful to you?"

"Common sense. There needs to be a great deal of initial caution and observation to determine that a particular medication does not unexpectedly cause a problem. Every medication that you take needs to be treated with respect. I never make an assumption about any medication until after someone has tried it."

"That makes a lot of sense."

"I think it does, but there's one other thing."

"What's that?"

"Any chemical can be harmful if you take too much of it, even water. And how much is too much is not the same for each person. So — bottom line — with any medication or herb or vitamin or food, if you have a side effect that is bothersome or potentially harmful, you should stop. You should proceed carefully at first in order that you don't exceed your own dose sensitivity. But all in all, with adults who take antidepressants without apparent side effects, I haven't had evidence of long-term damage."

Both Bradys were nodding.

I looked at Ben. "Have you had any noticeable problems since you've been on the Happox?"

"Nope."

"So what we know so far is that seven years of exposure to Happox for you seems to be okay. We still don't really know very long term how this might work out because Happox has only been around for about eleven years. And there are people who can't take it because of some side effect. But for many people like yourself, so far no major problems are emerging. So all we can say for now is that — for Ben — this medication is probably okay."

"Come to think of it, I might have one possible side effect."

"Which is?"

"Headaches. I rarely get headaches; but since

I've been on the Happox, I think they're a little more frequent. You know, I'm not even sure."

"Let's assume that is a side effect."

"Okay."

"You have obviously made some sort of judgment that you should continue the Happox despite the occasional headache."

"I guess I have."

"That's not unusual. Your situation may not be as clear as some, but I've had many patients who benefit dramatically from a medication who don't want to stop even if they do have a minimal side effect."

"So am I hurting myself to tolerate the headache and continue with the Happox?"

"Ben, I just don't know."

Lisa was smiling as she said, "There really is a lot you don't know."

I laughed. "Ignorance provides me with continuous opportunity to learn."

Ben also smiled but remained on track. "So side effects and long term damage are not necessarily connected."

"Right. Suppose you stop the Happox now after having seven years of medication experience with the possibility that you had an increased frequency of headaches. What I would expect to happen is that the headache frequency would diminish.

At that point, I would not expect that I could find any physical or laboratory abnormalities that would indicate that you ever took the Happox."

"Just as you wouldn't know if someone had taken a medication for high blood pressure and then stopped it."

"That's right, except the blood pressure elevation may have returned." I looked at the Bradys. "I know you would like definite answers, but they're not there. I try very hard not to be cavalier about the uncertainty." I hesitated. "Lisa, do you remember that I told you to stop any medication if you had a side effect?"

"Yes, I do."

"Do you remember what else I said?"

She thought for a moment and shook her head.

"I said even if you have no side effects, but intuitively didn't like the feeling that you had on that medication — even if you couldn't explain exactly why you felt that way — it was okay to stop."

"I remember."

"I like using intuition. Call it unscientific, but it's my small attempt to respect your body's wisdom and avoid substances which may be wrong for you, but not necessarily for another person."

"So we're constantly making educated guesses?"

"That's right. We just don't know about long term problems with anything that is relatively new, whether it's a medication, an herb, or even a new surgical procedure."

I could tell Lisa had her thinking cap on. "So if the potential downside, however small...."

I finished her sentence, "and however idiosyncratic, is really unknown, then why should we take the risk? Is that what you were about to say?"

"And what about that neuro-something you told me about, the way an antidepressant might help the brain to grow?"

"Neurogenesis?"

"That's the word?"

"What's that?" Ben asked.

"Well, it turns out that antidepressants may be a little bit like 'Miracle Grow' for the brain. The brain mood wiring may become a bit more robust with antidepressant fertilization. But that may also be true with some foods, physical exercise, or new learning."

"That's fascinating."

"That's exactly what Lisa said."

"Like Carl said, it's just 'food for thought.'" Lisa watched for Ben's reaction. He was quick on the uptake and smiled almost immediately.

"You'll hear more about this, I'm sure. But for now, let's just say that whether it is worth taking a medication is a cost benefit analysis. Most people seem to feel that the mood benefit they receive is

greater than the downside risk, which so far seems
minimal, especially if the medication feels right and
doesn't have any obvious side effects. This is especially true when somebody experiences intense
depression, which has significant mortality from
suicide. If you are one of those ten to fifteen percent
of people whose depression can become intense,
medication could save your life. But if you're one of
those individuals like you guys, whose depression is
less intense, it's more of a philosophical choice."

•• 19 ••

Preventive Medicine

"So what do you think about people like us?"

"You mean people with milder mood problems?"

"Yes."

"How esoteric and theoretical do you want me to be in answering that question?"

"Very."

"Okay. But first of all, there are two non-esoteric reasons to consider medication: quality of life and illness prevention. When you came in a few weeks ago, you mentioned that you were okay but not really feeling terrific. As you've responded to the medication, you've become happier. Perhaps you would say you're more creative, more energetic, more productive, more engaging, like your old self. And at times like this life seems to go better. Positive things happen."

"I think that's been true."

"So, many people ultimately choose to continue the medication because they feel they are more consistently happy and functioning closer to their best when they're on the medication. In the past, they may have achieved this good feeling and high level of function occasionally, but not with the consistency they experience with the medication. And it's that more consistent quality of life that they appreciate, so they decide not to stop."

"I can understand that."

"You wouldn't want ideal control of blood pressure or blood sugar or migraine to be intermittent or less than optimum, would you?"

"No."

"You'd want to have those medical problems under the most consistent optimum control possible. And that's exactly what I would try to do when I was treating those other medical problems as a family physician. So why should I not apply the same principle of adjustment to the mood system?"

Both nodded.

Ben said, "You also mentioned prevention."

"Yes. Let's turn the coin over. Most people ask questions about side effects or danger that occurs when they take a medication. I also like to consider the long-term "side effects" that might occur when somebody doesn't take a particular medication. For instance, what are the side effects of being significantly depressed, or even mildly depressed over the long haul? Is it not possible that there may be some other long-term physical problems which would be worse because of untreated depression?"

They both had a puzzled look.

"Suppose that you are depressed and you are exposed to a number of people who have colds. The chance that you'll catch a cold is greater if you're depressed than if you're feeling good emotionally. Immune system function is clearly better when somebody is not depressed. Not only do you fight infections better, there is the possibility that you may be more resistant to the development of cancer because your immune system is more efficient. Also, when someone is vulnerable to cardiac disease, to a heart attack for instance, the person will be at greater risk for the heart attack when depressed. I could go on, but the point is the mind-body connection is real, not just words. Other than smoking cessation or controlling blood pressure, I can't think of any other single health effort that would be more medically powerful in preventing illness than that of improving mood on a consistent basis."

Lisa had a surprised look. "That makes so much sense."

I nodded. "These preventive benefits are often overlooked." I looked at Ben, "You've been taking the Happox for seven years and I expect your experience has been positive or you wouldn't have continued."

He nodded.

"So isn't it ironic? Here you are without a tremendous personal resistance to taking medication, yet you were so embarrassed that you were reluctant to tell Lisa."

Ben grimaced and shook his head.

"I really feel badly about that."

"I didn't mean that as criticism. I think I understand how you feel — how both of you feel. But I hope you now understand that taking antidepressant medication is not a sign of character weakness any more than taking any other kind of medication is a sign of character weakness. "

"When you put it that way," Ben said, "It really makes sense, but it doesn't seem so esoteric. Where does the esoteric come in?"

"In part, it's what Lisa mentioned a few minutes ago, this concept of neurogenesis. The fact that neurons in the brain can develop new branching patterns with learning and other stimulation after childhood is very new information."

"You thought that wasn't the case?" Ben asked.

"That's right, we didn't know. Not only are there chemical variations between individuals, brain wiring and responsiveness may also vary from person to person; it's possible that people who are capable of depression may have more sensitivity to the influences that cause this growth or regression of certain brain areas that are important for mood."

"Are you implying that certain medications or other chemical substances may improve the brain's ability to change and adapt appropriately?" Lisa asked. "If some substances can make things worse, why couldn't some make things better?"

"That's what we're beginning to think. We're also finding that stress, or life experience, or psychological influence or whatever word you want to use actually can affect the way genes are expressed. This is called epigenetic modification and it's a very interesting concept."

Lisa seemed very engaged and she continued, "What about nutrition and medication, and what about maternal mood during pregnancy? Might all of that prove to be important in a positive as well as a negative way related to fetal development?"

I smiled, "You know, Ben, you have a very smart wife."

"I know," he smiled back.

Not to be distracted by our repartee, Lisa said, "So what's the answer."

"Well, it's another maybe. We're not certain, but it's not at all impossible that certain nutritional intervention during pregnancy, or mood improvement during pregnancy, could actually enhance fetal development. We do know that a high maternal stress level during pregnancy isn't good."

•• 20 ••

HOME ON THE [EMOTIONAL] RANGE

Lisa had taken Ben's hand. She said, "I'm determined to pin you down about something. Do you think that someone like me, and maybe Ben, is justified in taking medication if we can get along without it?"

I sighed, "I'd like to think that what I do enriches lives and improves health. With both of you I am inclined to think of medication as a reasonable part of that journey, an investment in personal potential, worth a try. But I don't feel wise enough to know when having a tinge of melancholy is valuable — maybe more valuable at that moment than being enriched. Maybe the coloration of life experience is in some way enhanced by that broader emotional bandwidth. Maybe the struggle with ups and downs contains seeds of personal growth. Maybe bumps in the road experienced during those times when life is flat or dissonant contribute to the richness of the soul and to creativity. For you guys, bal-

ancing these different values is very personal. I try
to help someone understand what I believe the process is all about. I want you to feel comfortable
about taking time to think through your situation,
maybe reviewing this a number of times."

"So again, you're not giving me a simple yes or
no – you should or you shouldn't take medication."

"I guess not."

It was then that Lisa embarrassed me,
"Would you stand up for a second?"

I didn't know what she was getting at, but I
stood up. She looked at Ben and winked, then she
stood up and gave me a big hug. I was really taken
by surprise. We sat down.

"Am I blushing?"

Ben laughed. "You're as red as a beet."

"I thought so."

"It's that mind-body thing."

"Right."

"That I understand, but I think I'm missing
something, and maybe you've said this early on and
I was not listening. You said something like the
experience of life might be enriched by that broader emotional bandwidth. What's emotional bandwidth?"

"I apologize, Ben. Lisa and I spoke about this
when she came in to see me a few weeks ago. Lisa,
do you mind if I go over this again with Ben?"

"Actually, I would like that."

"Good. What I meant is this, Ben: Amongst that unique, inherited mix of characteristics that makes up each of our temperaments is a particularly important attribute that I like to call affective bandwidth or emotional range. Those of us who are even-tempered have a relatively modest bandwidth, contained somewhere in the middle ground of that full spectrum of human emotion. Think of this as an area of emotional equilibrium. Even when provoked by psychological stress or hormonal imbalance or other internal chemical problems, the people who have inherited this even temperament have a resilient system and may experience only minimal depression. I believe this is not necessarily because they have more strength of character or willpower than the person who experiences the more serious depression; rather it's because they were born with protective physiology. So when someone comes to see me complaining of depression, I already suspect that they have an emotional range that goes beyond that middle even-temperedness. But what I've noticed is that those individuals who have a wider mood range usually have an upside as well as the down side. When that up side appropriately involves increased productivity and energy and enhances charisma, creativity, and confidence — whatever attributes you wish to apply — it's truly a blessing. I call it being affectively enriched. Okay so far?"

"Yep."

"So here's the irony. Those of us who have inherited even-temperedness have sort of a moderate range in the middle of the mood spectrum." I held my hands about a foot apart. "And those of us who have inherited the broader emotional range may have a little expansion," (I slid my hands about two feet apart) "or a more dramatic expansion" (I extended to full wing span). "It's at the most extreme that someone is called manic depressive or bipolar."

"Are you implying that the person who is even-tempered may not have that upside?" Ben asked.

"That's exactly what I'm implying."

"Really!"

"Really!" I smiled. " I asked Lisa to invite you here because I wanted to make sure that you understood what we were doing. I often do that."

"You mean invite a spouse?"

"Yes. There is so much misunderstanding that sometimes a spouse will be uneasy when their wife or husband takes medication. And it's ironic, but often the spouse will come in and proclaim that they are very even-tempered. When that's the case, I always ask the even-tempered spouse, 'Do you understand what your wife or husband is feeling when he or she is depressed? Do you appreciate her suffering?'"

"What do they say?"

"Almost always — No, I probably don't understand. I don't know why she doesn't just get up and try to do something to get going. I know she would feel better but she seems paralyzed.'"

"The fact is, many people don't understand what a significant or even relatively moderate depression feels like. But there may be a similar misunderstanding or lack of understanding about the upside, the affective enrichment. In the past few years I've begun to ask the even-tempered spouses not only about the depression, but also whether they have experienced the kind of exuberance and joy that they've seen their husband or wife experience. And guess what? I'm getting the same sort of response as I did when I asked the question about understanding depression. The husband or wife will say, 'Actually I don't think I really understand that either — sometimes I get jealous — I wish I could feel that way.'"

"You're saying that when the upside is not extreme, it's really a very good thing?"

"Does that strike you as unreasonable?"

Ben answered, "No, it's just a different way of looking at things." He hesitated. "What portion of the population is even-tempered and what portion has this wider emotional range or bandwidth that you're describing?"

"There is really no absolute number I can give or specific research that I'm aware of; but as an impression, I would say it's about fifty-fifty."

"Half being even-tempered and half having the wider bandwidth?" Lisa asked.

"I think so, but it's difficult to draw the line. The difference between a person who has a very modest widening of their emotional range and someone who is in that even-tempered or mood equilibrium group can be very minimal and arbitrary. But as the range expands, the differences become clearer. The problem in the past, however, was that most attention was paid to the more severe lows and especially to the more severe highs—the manic or near manic situation. Very little attention was paid to the wonderful and totally appropriate affective enrichment that is experienced by a substantial number of people." I suddenly hesitated, "Is it really fair to say that both of you have times of enrichment like those which I'm describing?"

Ben and Lisa looked at each other and then looked back at me and nodded yes. Ben said, "I think Lisa probably has a little more enrichment than I do, but for the most part you're absolutely right."

"I agree", Lisa added. She looked contemplative for a second and then continued, "Do you think that my more modest ups and downs are somehow related to my aunt's more extreme situation?"

"Possibly. I mentioned we don't inherit mood patterns and temperaments in cookie cutter fashion with identical symptoms, so your aunt's situation and your situation could have some relationship."

Ben joined in, "I thought I had read that about ten percent of the population is likely to become depressed?"

"That's a reasonable figure. I would probably say ten to fifteen percent of the population has the capacity to be seriously depressed."

"So if fifty percent, give or take, are even-tempered, and fifteen percent become seriously depressed, and one percent are manic-depressive, what happens to the other thirty or so percent?"

"Good question. That's the area that you and Lisa fit into. And there are an enormous number of people like you who go through life and experience ups and downs but without the intensity that would absolutely require treatment.

Lisa suddenly had a 'funny' look.

"What is it, Lisa?"

"Maybe this is a little bit off track, but I was wondering whether some people have an objection to taking this sort of medication because of their religious beliefs?"

"What do you mean?"

"Have you ever had someone say, 'God made me this way and maybe I shouldn't change what God did'?"

I nodded. "That does come up. And I absolutely respect someone's feeling in that regard, but it is interesting how rarely the same philosophical question comes up with hypertension."

"Meaning?"

"Meaning, with some obvious exceptions, there are probably fewer objections on religious grounds to taking medications for hypertension, or most other medical problems, than there is for depression."

Lisa smiled.

"You know, Lisa, this notion of being one's self, of not being altered, of being consistent with one's religious and spiritual beliefs is important, but why don't we consider intelligence, science, and intuition to be God-given? Where do we end? At our skin? Why not embrace our intellect and knowledge as part of us, as a growing dimension of our humanity?"

They both silently nodded, and Lisa said, "That's helpful."

"You're not the first person to raise the issue of religion or spirituality. In fact, there have been a growing number of studies about the power of prayer and intention in the healing process."

"With positive results?" Ben asked.

"With somewhat controversial positive results, which at this point in time are beyond the ability of science to explain."

·· 21 ··

THE FORTUNE 500

Lisa glanced at her watch, "I hate to bring us down to earth, but before we leave I have a practical question."

"What's that?"

"Should I put these visits through our insurance? I understand that the mere fact that you've seen a psychiatrist can create problems obtaining certain kinds of insurance."

"Unfortunately that's often true."

"In addition, when I read our insurance policy to understand our coverage..."

Ben interrupted, "Before we get into that, honey, could I clear up something?"

Lisa broke into a broad smile and shook her head. "Sure. You know, I really can't believe I was worried about you coming here tonight."

Ben smiled, "I was probably more worried than you."

I waited just a moment, "So, what's your

question?"

"Since Lisa can be a little more up and down than me, I take it her mood range is wider than mine?"

"Could be."

"I was also thinking...." He glanced at Lisa as he was speaking.

"Say what you're thinking."

"Well, I'm thinking that your mood range is not only wider than mine, but somehow you're a little moodier as well."

"You mean my moods go up and down more easily?"

"Yes."

Lisa smiled. "I think you're right."

"And I think I know where you're headed, Ben."

"That's good because I'm not sure I do."

"I'll put it this way, you both agree that Lisa has a broader bandwidth?"

"Yes." In unison.

"And you both would agree that Lisa's mood platform has more grease, more lubrication, that her moods change more easily?"

The Bradys glanced at each other, "That's an interesting way to put it, but I certainly think it's descriptive."

"Well, there are a lot of attributes that con-tribute to the uniqueness of each person's tempera-

ment. Mood range and mood lubrication are two of
three very important characteristics that I always
try to understand in order to make choices about
the medication or approach I may take in trying to
help someone."

"What is the third important characteristic?"
Ben asked.

"I call it the thermostat or the Fortune Five
Hundred factor."

"What's that?"

"We all seem to have a thermostat that deter-
mines a kind of default setting — the place where
our mood tends to stay much of the time."

"Like I might tend to be a little more middle
ground and Lisa might usually be slightly upbeat?"

"Yes. That's exactly what I mean."

"So with Lisa and me...."

"I would tend to say that Lisa has a slightly
broader bandwidth, that she tends to run a bit more
enriched, but you're steadier. She cycles her moods
more."

"Very interesting." Lisa said. "And you think
these characteristics are genetically determined?"

"Probably, at least in part."

"So what does all this have to do with the
Fortune Five Hundred?" Ben asked.

"Maybe nothing," I smiled. "But I'll tell you my
theory, and this is not a scientific study. My per-

centages are pie in the sky based on my general impressions."

They both nodded.

"As I said before, probably half the world is even-tempered, and about half the world to a greater or lesser degree has a wider mood range. Most people who have a wider emotional range don't live at the extremes but spend much of the time in the equilibrium middle ground, or maybe being a little bit down or dissonant."

"Sort of determined by their thermostat?"

"Right, and a few lucky souls seem to have a thermostat set on enriched that keeps them above average mood wise. I consider them to have a high E.Q.—emotional quotient."

"The equivalent to the high I.Q.?"

"Right. They're almost always energetic, enthusiastic, engaged, charismatic, creative, productive, gregarious, happy — great to be around."

They both nodded.

Ben asked, "A small number?"

I nodded.

"How small?"

"Again, pie in the sky, but I'm guessing between three and five percent of the population is blessed in this way. And here's where the Fortune Five Hundred comes in. If I had the opportunity to interview all of the men and women who are CEO's of

the Fortune Five Hundred companies, I would
expect at most about five percent or therefore twenty-five of those CEO's to be blessed with this sort of
consistent affective enrichment. I suspect, however,
that I would find perhaps a hundred-and-fifty to
two-hundred CEO's who fit this description." I hesitated. "I have a feeling that these high achieving
individuals are bright and intelligent, but their real
advantage comes from running on eight emotional
cylinders almost all the time."

"Boy, does that make sense." Ben paused. "I
know a few people like that. And actually, although
I couldn't have put this into words before tonight,
since I've been taking the medication I think the
main change is that I am consistently slightly
enriched as opposed to staying pretty much in a
middle ground."

Before I could respond, Lisa said, "That's also a
pretty good description of the way I've been feeling."

I nodded. I glanced at my watch and suddenly
felt tired.

"I know it's late," Lisa said.

"We probably should call it an evening," I said.
"But let's get back to your concerns about
insurance."

·· 22 ··

ASSHOLISTIC HEALTHCARE

1   "I was saying that I read our insurance policy last week and I was really surprised, maybe shocked is a better word."

"Explain."

5   "Well, I guess I was already annoyed. A few months ago our son David needed some medical tests, and obtaining approval to have them done was like pulling teeth. It was ridiculous. So when I read about the mental health coverage in our poli-

10   cy, I was even more aggravated. In fact, I thought I must have misunderstood and I called the insurance company."

"And?"

"I hadn't misunderstood."

15   "What do you mean, honey?"

"Carl happens to be on our list of psychiatrists or it would be even worse, but our co-pay for any visit is fifty percent of the charge, while the co-pay for other doctor visits in any other specialty is only twenty percent."

"Really?"

"Yes. And listen to this. Each year we have a thousand dollars of coverage for outpatient psychiatry, and unbelievably only two thousand dollars for inpatient coverage should we need hospitalization. That's probably not going to be an issue with us, but still…. How long would that two thousand dollars last?"

"Blink your eyes." I responded.

"What happens then?" Ben asked.

"Simple, you're liable for the bill. And that's not easy for most people, so the hospital becomes nervous. They put pressure on doctors to get people in and out quickly before the insurance runs out."

The Bradys shook their heads.

"And even if there were more coverage than you have in your particular policy, someone in the insurance company, not necessarily a physician, may decide that the hospitalization is not according to 'standards' or is somehow inappropriate and refuse authorization. If there is an appeal, it is often after the fact. Insurance companies say they're not practicing medicine, but there's no way this process doesn't impact and distort medical decision-making. I'm not saying that cost control isn't important, but with the current insurance and malpractice environment, the very nature of medical practice has been altered. For doctors, it's terribly demoralizing. As a group, in the context of their professional work, doctors are depressed! The joy, the interest, the passion, the doctor-patient relationship.... It's so sad, especially if you've watched the change over time as I have. Privately, I've been thinking of what we have now as the era of 'Assholistic Healthcare', or maybe it should be called 'Meshuganah Medicine'. And most of the problems come from outside the medical profession."

"What's Meshuganah?"

"It's a Yiddish word meaning a kind of bumbling ineptitude – always managing to screw things up in a way."

"And you see medicine that way?"

"Healthcare is an absolute mess. It's so fragmented and disorganized and irrational that it reminds me of the Tower of Babel. I've even wondered if it's ethical for doctors to agree to practice medicine in this environment – where insurance companies, for all intents and purposes, put us in the compromised position of making medical choices for patients that in our heart of hearts we believe are not necessarily in their best interest. "

"Why don't doctors rise up?"

"Good question. They say getting doctors to agree to something is like herding cats."

Lisa laughed.

"But I think the real problem is that the medical profession as a whole, and doctors individually, feel professionally impotent. "

"What do you mean?" Ben asked.

"When someone or some entity feels they have lost control of their direction or decision making, there is a kind of demoralization and lassitude that sets in. As I've said, Insurance policy distorts medical decision making, and medical malpractice not only drives doctors away from practice for financial reasons, but the growth of this litigious industry over the past fifty years is a malignancy that has driven a wedge between doctor and patient, and torn the fabric of this crucial relationship that used to be the cornerstone of medical care. I love helping people, but I am extremely saddened by what has happened in the more than forty years since I walked into medical school.

"Wow!" Lisa spoke the word softy. She smiled, "Maybe you should write a book called 'Assholistic Healthcare.'"

"At first blush, that feels too overwhelming to even contemplate."

"Well, I mean it. Just this little glimpse that I have gotten into your profession shows me what a real mess it is. When I spoke to our insurance company, I asked about the hospital limitations. I asked whether there would be any similar limitation if I was hospitalized for pneumonia or diabetes or a heart attack."

"And?"

"There was far more liberal coverage for hospital care related to every other category of illness."

"So, you're saying that mental health is really mired in Assholistic Healthcare."

"I am," Lisa smiled. "Yes, I am."

"Do you know if your policy has a lifetime cap for mental health?"

"Oh, yes, I forgot to mention that. We have only twenty thousand dollars of lifetime coverage for inpatient or outpatient mental healthcare. But with other illnesses, the cap is one million dollars."

"Do you mean that once we spend twenty thousand dollars for mental healthcare, we are no longer covered?"

"Exactly."

"Really?" Ben looked surprised.

"Yes."

"How can they do that?" Ben seemed genuinely annoyed.

I responded. "Ben, insurance companies have been historically prejudiced where mental health is concerned. And now, even though there is increasing awareness that mental health problems are medical just like everything else, the insurance companies don't want to put mental health on the same playing field because they don't want to give up those dollars that they have historically not paid. The irony is that they're shortsighted. There have been studies that demonstrate that when you take care of the mental health needs of people, the actual cost of all medical services declines because visits to other doctors decline."

"Do the insurance companies know that?"

"I'm sure that information has been presented, but there is so much pressure these days to cut medical costs that the notion of giving ground and increasing mental health benefits just goes against the grain. Discrimination against mental health has been going on for years. There has been some increased movement towards parity, but who knows?" I hesitated. "Maybe it's because I have been on both sides of a very inappropriate fence that I see things the way I do. So many patients and even other physicians think of psychiatry as being 'out there' — floating in space in some milky way of craziness. Although the understanding of psychiatry has evolved a lot since those days in 1981 when I walked down Main Street in Bennington, many people still experience a sense of stigma or shame when they have to see a 'shrink.' Psychiatry is still a place that many physicians send people when they don't have a medical clue what else to do with them. 'It's all in your head.'" I smiled, "Damn right it's all in your head, but not the way they mean. What happens in the mind is very medical, and mind-body medicine is very real." I sighed and shook my head. "Mental health - what happens in your mind — should not be viewed as some abstract aberration which is a reflection of weakness of will or character. It should be seen for what it is, a component of medicine which is very much at the center of health."

Ben was shaking his head. "Sad — Isn't there some sort of antidepressant for the for the profession?"

I began to smile. "Well, it seems that a coalition of esteemed philosophical chemists have devised a wonderful medicine called Imsense, which is a true antidote to Assholistic Healthcare, but they can't get it through the FDA."

Lisa began to laugh. "Imsense?"

"Yes, that's short for intelligent medicine that makes sense."

Lisa took the bait and continued smiling, "How does it work?"

"As soon as you put it in your mouth it causes malpractice reform; once swallowed, it provides coverage for medication costs of older individuals. Upon hitting the stomach, doctors regain control of medical decision making; and as it traverses the intestines it eliminates the Tower of Babel insurance network and substitutes a rational coherent cover-age system which leaves no one out."

"Sounds like quite a pill. What objections does the FDA have?" Lisa's smile was huge.

I began to laugh, "Insufficient side effects."

We were all smiling; but it really wasn't funny.

·· 23 ··

BRAINS

Lisa looked as though she was about to stand – but suddenly became still. "I was supposed to ask you about counseling." She turned to Ben, "I asked Carl whether he thought I should be in counseling and he said, 'If I thought it would help, but it wasn't urgent.'"

I nodded. "Let me give you a more complex answer than I gave you on the phone."

"Okay."

I hesitated, scratched my chin, and thought for a moment. "Lisa, do you know what a placebo response is?"

"Sure, it's a false response to a fake pill."

I smiled, "That's exactly what I hoped you'd say."

"But I'm wrong."

"You are wrong."

"Why?"

"Let me answer that after I give Ben a one-minute primer about his health system."

"What do you mean?" Ben asked.

"You and I and Lisa take care of most of our own medical needs without doctors or pills. We're continually manufacturing our own internal drugs."

"You mean…"

"Hormones, neurotransmitters, digestive chemicals, enzymes – whatever."

"Interesting."

"And we dispense these medications internally as we need them."

Ben nodded.

"So, in your brain, if you came into this appointment anxious because of what you feared you would have to tell Lisa, and now you are relieved – I believe your internal brain drugs have self-adjusted and led you to feel better."

"So there's been a real change in my brain chemistry?"

"Yes. The changes in how we feel don't occur in the abstract. They are the result of chemical changes in your brain."

"I hadn't thought about it that way, but it makes sense."

"So – in almost any research study involving a new antidepressant medication, about thirty percent of patients receiving a so-called placebo feel better."

"Okay."

"I believe that some people who receive placebo have a gift of being able to self-prescribe their own internal antidepressants. That's why they feel a real change in mood."

"Why would that happen?"

"My guess is that they have a surge of hope and some of that 'internal blushing' occurs in their brain and they self-prescribe."

"How do you know this?"

"Because of the remarkable advances in functional brain imaging, allowing us to look inside the brain and watch it work; we can compare the changes in placebo response with the changes that occur with taking the antidepressant medication. I'm not sure this represents every situation in which there is a placebo response, but at least some of them."

"But it doesn't last."

"What doesn't last?"

"Compared to the antidepressant medication effect, the placebo response doesn't last."

"Right, it usually tails off after some weeks. But you know what might not tail off after a few weeks?"

Ben made no reply.

"The effect of effective counseling."

Lisa had been listening. "So, that's where you're going?"

"Where?"

"You're about to say that counseling also changes our brain chemistry."

"I mentioned that to you before, but that's exactly what I was about to say to Ben."

"But after you stop counseling, wouldn't the changes fade away?"

"Not necessarily, Ben. If the therapy leads to a more or less permanent change in your internal representation of the world, an altered and improved brain chemical response to different situations may persist; that's especially true if you refresh your therapy with an occasional visit or relevant reading. Some neuroscientists now describe medication changes as improvements in brain function from the 'bottom up.' In other words, the medication affects deeper brain structures involved with the adjustment of emotion and those deeper structures affect the cortex where conscious thinking occurs."

Before I could continue, Lisa pre-empted me again, "And therapy is change from the top down."

I looked at Lisa and she knew what I was thinking. "Well, I know a little about the brain from some courses I had in college, and if the therapy is effective in altering thinking, I guess it could change chemical reactions deeper in the brain through various connections."

I laughed, "You're too much."

Ben was smiling. "It's difficult to live with someone so smart."

Lisa gave him a mock punch on the arm. Then Ben asked, "So wouldn't it be better in almost every instance to do counseling?"

"It probably wouldn't hurt. But I've found through the years that counseling especially helps when there are difficult problems in someone's background, or difficult immediate circumstances that need to be worked through. Lisa was pretty lucky because she grew up without much psychologic trauma and her family was relatively normal, something that is pretty rare. When Lisa lost her custody case, it probably dealt a *coup d'gras* to her internal mood chemistry; but as I said to her, I didn't think she would benefit from counseling around that issue. I may have been wrong, but I felt medication was more likely to help."

"Is there ever a time that you would suggest counseling and not use medication?" Lisa asked.

"Good question. In your case, for instance, you can function reasonably well without medication. So if you decided to continue with medication it would only be if you thought there is some long-term improvement in the quality of your life. In fact, you and Ben are both in that elective boat."

"So you're saying that Lisa could get along without medication and without therapy."

"Yes, in her situation I believe both treatments are elective."

Lisa turned to Ben, "Carl and I spoke more about this last time and I'll explain when we get home."

"Okay."

"I know you guys are tired, but I have to add one more comment to my answer. Lisa, If you asked me six months ago whether there were any situations in which I would use therapy and not medication, I would have probably said no. But based on some new brain research, I might now be inclined to treat certain problems by first trying therapy before resorting to medication; some people can make those therapy-generated top down improvements that seem persistent without requiring medication. In your situation, therapy alone might not cut it, I just wanted to mention that possibilities and perspectives are changing because of the remarkable rocket-like expansion of knowledge about brain function and genetics."

The Bradys nodded – looking very tired. Ben said, "I guess there's one thing that bothers me, and that is the notion that how we perceive the world can be so changeable and responsive to the mood that we're in. It's a little disconcerting to think of reality that way.

"Ben, Lisa and I spoke about this last time and

I quoted from John Milton, 'The mind is its own place, and in itself, can make a heaven of hell, and a hell of heaven.' I think Lisa felt we were very 'perceptually fragile.' I turned to Lisa, "Is that right?"

"I think so."

·· 24 ··

Ignorance

Iglanced at the recessed lights in the ceiling; they were probably not turned on full but I liked the feeling. I looked at the Bradys. "You know, we probably should call it a night. I'm tired and I'm sure both of you are."

Lisa responded, "I'm beat, but this was very worthwhile. Thanks so much for taking all of this time."

"You're welcome." I hesitated. "I want to emphasize one thing. Remember when I said this discussion was food for thought, not gospel?"

"Yes."

"I think the perspectives that I've shared with you are reasonable, but there's much more we don't know than we do. I've said before that we doctors forget just how much we really don't know." I paused, "Just look around this room. There are colors in here we can't see because our eyes aren't capable of perceiving the full color spectrum."

Lisa said, "Hmm," as though she connected.

"There's also music in the room that we can't hear."

The only obvious sound at that moment was a rattle coming from the air conditioning duct in the ceiling. I swiveled my chair turning to the left, looking through the piles of mail, articles, and charts cluttering my desk. I finally found the remote control for a small stereo that was sitting on the floor in a corner of the room. I knew the radio was set to a local jazz station. I pressed power and the sweet sounds of a saxophone filled the air. "The point is, the music is always here but we can't hear it; the colors are here and we can't see them; and these are just the limitations of our senses! What are the limitations of our comprehension? What don't we understand?" I didn't expect an answer. "Maybe in fifty years these ideas I've been sharing with you about mood and emotion will seem ludicrous. I don't think that's the case, but I'm sure George Washington's doctors thought they were correct when they applied leeches and bled him to near death."

Silence for a moment. We all looked at each other and then Lisa said, "I appreciate what you're saying." She paused and glanced upward. "You know, I've never forgotten a line from a play I read in college." Her eyes became moist. "I don't know why I'm choking up." She reached over and extracted a tissue from the box on the sofa's arm and dabbed. When her face emerged her eyes were a little bloodshot but dry. Ben put his arm around her shoulder.

"So what's the line?" I asked quietly.

She glanced upward again for a split second as if remembering, then said, "The play was 'The Life of Galileo' by Bertold Brecht, and the line was 'Truth is the child of time, not of authority.'"

Ben's face turned red and Lisa was immediately aware. She bent towards her husband and kissed him gently on the cheek. "I didn't mean it that way, honey."

"I'm sorry."

"It's really okay."

"And I really like your quote, Lisa."

A smile crept over her recently moist face. "So there's a lot you're really not sure about."

"Bingo!"

The three of us laughed. Still smiling, Lisa said, "In all seriousness, I won't take you too seriously. But I will wave to you on Main Street."

I smiled. "Good."

PART IV

IDEA INDEX

Idea Index

Most people read the first edition of this book quickly and easily, but a surprising minority read the book a second time. I asked 'Why?' The answer I generally received was "During the first reading I was 'listening' to the conversation. During the second reading, I really had more focus on the ideas." It was great that some people were motivated enough to read the book twice, but I knew not everybody would do that. I wanted to find a way that would allow someone to review a topic without having to review the whole book. Thus, this **Idea Index** was born.

The **Index** is separated into sixteen topics, which were explicitly mentioned or inferred during my conversations with Lisa and Ben. Under each topic, the **Index** references conversation by chapter, page and line if necessary. In a few instances, I have used the Index as an opportunity to expand on the discussion of a particular topic in the text.

As I said to the Bradys on a number of occasions, the ideas I have shared may be reasonable at this time, but ultimately may prove to be untrue or only partially true; fortunately, over the years the growing body of scientific evidence has been supportive.

Affective Bandwidth (Inherited Mood Range)

As a noun, affect is defined as emotion or feeling. There is a nascent trend in Psychiatry to substitute Affective Spectrum Disorder (ASD) for the more commonly used terms of depression, dysthymia, euthymia, cyclothymia, hypomania, and mania. My own inclination is towards the development of a new nomenclature using "Affective Spectrum Variation" (ASV) because this designation may somewhat reduce the pejorative cast that is attached to our current nomenclature, and may better reflect the fluidity, nuance and individuality that characterize each person as unique.

Practically speaking, whatever words we use, I believe that as part of temperament we each inherit a fairly specific affective bandwidth (emotional range) that more or less defines how far down emotionally (depressed) or how far up emotionally (enriched) each of us is capable of achieving. I also believe there are many among us whose moods are consistently midrange and comfortable without any extremes (even-tempered). This notion of bandwidth has important implications for treatment.

Chapter 4 – Normal?

Whole chapter

Because of genetics I always try to get a sense of affective
bandwidth in other family members, whether or not these
family members ever had a formal mental health diagnosis.

Chapter 7 – Affective Bandwidth

Read the entire Chapter. This is the core primer on
Affective Bandwidth.

Chapter 9 – To Take or Not To Take? (That is the Question)

P 67   *1-16*

Lisa's aunt's presumed diagnosis was Bipolar I or
Manic Depressive illness, which refers to individuals
with the broadest or most extreme affective bandwidth.

Chapter 20 – Home On The [Emotional] Range

Pp 140-145

P 146   *1-8*

Chapter 21 – The Fortune 500

Pp 150-153

Affective Enrichment
(The "Understudied" Holy Grail)

I give special attention to *affective enrichment* because it is too rarely considered by professionals unless an individual is excessively enriched and becomes hypomanic or manic. Paying greater attention to *enrichment* might have significant implications for *optimal* treatment.

One professional who has paid attention is Dr. Kaye Redfield Jamison. In her recent book **Exuberance** *(Affective Enrichment?)* she writes, "We have given sorrow many words, but passion for life few...I believe that exuberance is incomparably more important than we acknowledge. If, as it had been claimed, enthusiasm finds the opportunities and energy makes the most of them, the mood of mind that yokes the two is formidable indeed. Exuberant people take in the world and act upon it differently than those who are less lively and less energetically engaged. They hold their ideas with passion and delight, and act upon them with dispatch. Their love of life and adventure is palpable."

Chapter 4 – Normal?

Because of genetics, I always try to get a sense of affective enrichment/bandwidth in other family members, whether or not they have ever had a formal diagnosis.

	P 19	*22-23*
	P 21	*11-15*
	P26	*11-28*
	P 27	*1-2*

Chapter 7 – Affective Bandwidth

	P 51	*14-19*
	P 53	*1-2*
	P 54	*27-28*
	P 55	*1-17*
	P 56	*14-28*
	P 57	*1-12*

Chapter 20 – Home On The [Emotional] Range

	Pp 142-145

Chapter 21 – The Fortune 500

	P 151	*7-28*
	P 152	
	P 153	*1-21*

Assholistic Healthcare

It has been more than forty years since I entered medical school. Over the course of those years, (it's my impression) the science of medicine has improved while actual medical care and caring have declined. I DO NOT believe physicians are the primary culprits in our unfortunate, sad and sometimes asinine healthcare environment. In the United States today, we do not have a true healthcare system; we have a government dominated, demoralizing, irrational national semi-public, semi-private mess.

Chapter 11 – A Few Days Later		
	P 92	*7-18*
Chapter 22 – Assholistic Medicine		
	Whole Chapter	

Chemical Imbalance
(Biological/Medical Psychiatry)

Almost all medical problems require chemical imbalance. In the brain, our incredibly unique palate of mood, energy, emotion and cognition depends upon unique variations of chemistry and/or anatomy. Although psychological stress is important and impacts all medical problems (including depression, anxiety, mania, schizophrenia, etc.), stress does not cause the medical problem *unless the individual has sufficient genetic vulnerability to develop the chemical imbalance related to that particular medical problem in the first place.*

Chapter 5 – Chicken or Egg?		
	Whole Chapter	
Chapter 9 – To Take or Not To Take? (That is the Question)		
	P 72	*10-28*
	P 73	
Chapter 12 – Rash Decisions		
	P 94	
	P 95	*1-2*
Chapter 14 – Sugar & Spice & Stainless Steel		
	P 107	*4-26*

Elective Psychiatry
(The Interface Of Philosophy And Healthcare)

Since I've been practicing medicine, the number of "pills" on the market for all sorts of medical conditions has vastly increased. Also, the laboratory thresholds for treating diabetes, cholesterol, and hypertension have dropped, meaning that millions of people are now being offered "pills" who would not have been offered "pills" in earlier times.

Furthermore, the advances in brain science have been so prolific, that there has been an especially obvious proliferation of "pills" in psychiatry.

In any specialty, medicines which idiosyncratically cause side effects should not be taken by that patient. Also, any medication which substantially carries inherent risks for a significant swath of patients should not be approved by the FDA. So, I ask you, is the availability of more treatment options (including more pills) a bad thing?

My personal and professional health strategy has been sculpted by my medical education and experience, but is inevitably prejudiced by my personal life experiences. However, the information in this book is not intended as advocacy, just "food for thought" (which I mentioned to Lisa many times). Lisa did not *have* to take medication, she *chose* to. It was okay with me if she didn't.

Because of culturally conflicted perspectives, the expanded use of "pills" for cholesterol, blood pressure, sugar control, or whatever, has been and will continue to be less controversial than the use of "pills" in psychiatry.

Specifically, should we provide medication to people like Lisa, who have functioned reasonably well without our help? Even more controversial might be the notion of improving the cognitive mental function of people who already are functioning in a 'normal' fashion.

Idiosyncrasy

Medication (indeed any treatment) works or doesn't work in the context of a particular person. It has been my impression that medical education does not emphasize uniqueness of response with enough intensity. There is an implicit perspective that a medication does certain things and works a certain way at a given dose with most (if not all) patients. It has been my observation as both a family physician and psychiatrist that people are often far more unpredictable in their response to a given medication than our training would have us believe.

If a physician insists that a medication he or she prescribed should not work in the way you describe, or does not cause the side effect that you complain of, (in my experience) the physician is usually wrong (for you), and you are usually correct (and not overreacting).

Integrative Pluralism
(The Need To Not Oversimplify)

It is no longer acceptable to think in terms of a single cause for anything in mental health. Every person is unique. Every mental variation is multifactorial with relation to genetics, psychology, personal circumstance, chemistry, anatomy, infectious agents, principles of physics, and other influences about which we are as yet ignorant. In an article entitled "Toward A Philosophical Structure For Psychiatry" (American Journal of Psychiatry; March 2005) Kenneth Kendler writes, "Psychiatric disorders are etiologically complex, and we can expect no more 'spirokete-like' discoveries that will explain their origins in simple terms. Explanatory pluralism is preferable to monastic explanatory approaches, especially biological reductionism. Psychiatry needs to move from a pre-scientific 'battle of paradigms' toward a more mature approach that embraces complexity along with empirically rigorous and pluralistic explanatory models. Finally, we need to accept 'patchy reductionism' with the goal of piecemeal integration in trying to explain the complex etiologic pathways to psychiatric illness a little bit at a time."

I realize that's a mouthful, but what an elegant mouthful it is. However, there is one bit of irony worth noting.

Dr. Kendler spoke of "spirokete-like discoveries," alluding to the mental health ravages of neurosyphilis in the pre-antibiotic era. I would like to shine a special spotlight on infectious agents as part of the pluralistic environment.

I strongly suspect that we will find a pervasive involvement of microorganisms that act as vectors (in conjunction with other factors such as genetic variability) to trigger all sorts of medical problems in susceptible individuals. For example, a bacteria (H. pylori) is found in the stomachs of a significant number of people who develop gastric ulcers. However, some ulcers occur without H. pylori and some people with H. pylori do not develop ulceration. "Cold viruses" are more likely to induce the development of upper respiratory infections in individuals whose immune system can't fight them off; Tourette's syndrome, rheumatic heart disease, and certain forms of kidney disease have all been associated with exposure to bacteria. M.S. (multiple sclerosis) and Insulin Dependent Diabetes may be triggered by viral exposure in genetically vulnerable individuals. With syphilis, might there have been some individuals back in the day who were genetically able to resist the spirokete's destructive power, while other individual's immune systems were not up to the task? The simple message that Dr. Kendler is conveying, "Let's not over simplify."

Mind-Body Medicine

The mind is a construct of awareness and creativity. "It" is largely brain dependent, but not an exact equivalent. The brain is a part of our body, interdependent with all other parts, but clearly the commander-in-chief. Thus, mind-body medicine implies an inter-reactivity of not only the mind and the liver, stomach and pancreas, but also the mind and the brain.

Nature versus Nurture (Heredity vs. Environment)

It's not either/or – it's both. You do need two to tango, but one partner leads the dance. Over the years I have become increasingly convinced that the lead partner is ...nature.

Chapter 5 – Chicken or Egg?		
	Pp 39-40	
	P 41	*1-12*
Chapter 6 – Blue Genes		
	Whole Chapter	
Chapter 8 – Medication		
	P 62	*22-28*
	P 63	*1-11*
This is the "nature part" of the equation.		
Chapter 9 – To Take or Not To Take? (That is the Question)		
	P 67	*5-15*
Chapter 14 – Sugar & Spice & Stainless Steel		
	P 103	*8-28*
	Pp 104-106	
	P 107	*1-3*

Neurogenesis

Until very recently, prevailing wisdom suggested that the brain stopped growing past childhood or adolescence. We now know that is not correct.

Actual new brain cells may develop in adulthood; also existing cells can develop more branches and new circuitry, becoming more robust. That robustness may translate into greater operational efficiency in certain areas of the brain, including areas that regulate mood and emotion.

Some of the beneficial action of brain medications that I prescribe every day may actually work in part because they stimulate neurogenesis (a sort of "Miracle-Grow" for the brain).

Chapter 11 – A Few Days Later		
	P 90	*14-28*
	P 91	
	P 92	*1-6*
Chapter 18 - Idiosyncrasy		
	P 132	*9-23*
Chapter 19 – Preventive Medicine		
	P 137	*19-28*
	P 138	*1-14*

Neuromodulation

Currently, as a professional term of art in medicine, neuromodulation is being used in a very specific way – to address a growing number of electric/magnetic treatments, which adjust and enhance brain chemistry and function. Approved treatments include ECT (electroconvulsive therapy) and VNS (vagal nerve stimulation). Investigational treatments include rTMS (repetitive Transcranial Magnetic Stimulation) or DBS (Deep Brain Stimulation).

I personally believe anything that leads to an adjustment of brain chemistry (talk therapy, casual conversation, non-casual conversation, acupuncture, exercise, meditation, medication – indeed all ingested and non-ingested treatments) could be included under the neuromodulation umbrella.

In the "big picture," if psychiatry had a tag line, it might be, *"neuromodulation – it's what we do."*

Preventive Medicine

Individuals who suffer from depression and other significant affective problems are generally less healthy when they are depressed. There is increasing evidence that the existence of significant depression enhances vulnerability to cardiac events, cancer, infectious disease, and many other medical maladies to *which a given individual is vulnerable.* Therefore, the treatment of medical affective illness (depression et. al.) is a powerful preventive medicine strategy.

I'm always a bit bemused by questions raised about long-term side effects of medications. I often ask the question, "What do you believe would have greater negative consequences and side effects – the consumption of a medication which has no obvious side effects and obviously improves affective function for ten years, or the existence of a significant depression over ten years?" Most people smile with clarity when they think about the answer to that question.

In psychiatry specifically there is a growing sense that early intervention will moderate the course of schizophrenia, depressive and bipolar illnesses. (The jury is still out.) If this impression is substantially confirmed, there will be difficult decisions with regard to "labeling" a child or a young adult with what is considered to be a serious and uncomfortable diagnosis, but it may be in their long-term best interest to do so.

Chapter 19 – Preventive Medicine
Whole Chapter

Stigma and Misunderstanding (Psychiatry is the "Rodney Dangerfield" (I don't get no respect) of Specialties)

In case you did not read the preface to this book, here it is. "Many people, including some physicians, just don't understand psychiatry. I became all too aware of this when I switched to psychiatry after years of family practice and emergency medicine. At its best, psychiatry's core is the mystery of our humanness. It is not some eccentric abstraction that denotes craziness or weakness; nor it is a repository for patients whose problems seem to have no obvious answers. The condescending phrase, 'It's all in your head' makes me crazy (excuse the expression). With all due respect and with as much sophistication as our ignorance will allow, it may not be all in our heads; however, in a very real and positive sense, much of it is."

Suicide and Other Side Effects (All treatment cause side effects – the issue is not whether they will occur, but what you do when they happen)

Early on, I asked Lisa about suicide. She denied this as a problem (for her) and I believed her. Recently, there has been increased concern as to whether antidepressants could cause a child (or adult) to suicide. In my discussion with Lisa, especially on page 65, I instruct her to feel free to stop medication immediately, not only if there are side effects, but also if her intuition alone suggests that the medication is not good (for her).

I instruct all my patients this way. I do so because in many instances a particular antidepressant will not work for that individual, and in rare instances an antidepressant can unpredictably make things worse. In that instance, if the antidepressant is not stopped quickly, it might theoretically provoke a suicidal response. *In my judgment, therefore, the issue of suicide risk to a large extent reflects patient management involving close follow-up, rather than the inevitability of rare idiosyncratic reactions to antidepressants (or any chemical, medication, nutriceutical, or food substance).*

I believe that far more people are helped by taking medication than are hurt by taking medication. I also believe that some people lose out by not taking medication.

Chapter 8 – Medication		
	P 64	*25-28*
	P 65	*1-15*
Chapter 9 – To Take or Not To Take? (That is the Question)		
	P 69	*20-28*
	P 70	
Chapter 11 – A Few Days Later		
	P 84	*27-28*
	P 85	
	P 86	*1-23*

The rare exacerbation of suicidal behavior by an antidepressant is often preceded by days or weeks of worsening feelings.

By allowing a patient to stop a medication if it doesn't "feel right", suicidal impulses may be prevented.

Treatments – (Ingested)

Please remember that anything we ingest and digest is a chemical. This includes food, vitamins, herbs, nutriceuticals, homeopathic remedies, and medication.

Treatments – (Non-Ingested)

I thought of identifying treatments as "chemical" and "non-chemical." I realized, however, that many if not all of so call non-chemical treatments may work (at least in part) by provoking internal chemical change in our brain (and body).

SUPPORT AND CONTINUING EDUCATION

If you are interested in continued information about the topics in this book, please contact me at www.stantonandsamuel.com.

ACKNOWLEDGMENTS

Many patients, colleagues and friends helped with the evolution of this book and offered suggestions that were very helpful. I am grateful to all.

I owe very special thanks to: Diane Volmer and Kathy Goldstein for their patience, skill and perspective as they typed and re-typed this book; Connie Rubinstein, my journalist sister, Nancy Shils, my sister-in-law (who defies easy description), and Barry Shils, my filmmaker brother-in-law, for their advice and wisdom; Jeff Davies and Ed Massey of Ponte Vedra Beach, Florida; my good friends Dale Guldbrandsen and Sally Mole of Manchester, Vermont; editor Judy Steen; Dennis D'Arienzo, Jack McNeil, and Denise McDonald of Stanton and Samuel Publishing, for all their help and support.

I've also been blessed with a wonderful professional home. In addition to myself, there are seven other professionals who enrich this environment -- David Blackmon, my wife Ronnie Burak, Jamie Fletcher, Deb Hardman, Naomi Jacobs, Ron Kirsner and Mercedes McGowan, all contributing in various measure to the emotional torture of our truly great staff. Our sitcom would be called "Monday to Friday Live" if only we had the chutzpah and time to hurdle HIPPA and write things down.

The "Monday to Friday" crew over these nine years has included some fabulous humorists whose lives have been indelibly distorted by being part of this group. With condolences, I give my sincere thanks to Dawn Coen, Debbie Halpin, Penny Carpenter, Judy Eads, Zel Story, Tamara Walker, Sandy Kelly, Lisa Spencer, Robin Ford, Dana Hooper, Shelly Oliff, Ursula Vargas, and last but certainly not least Francey Green. This group has always supported me and immensely buoyed my spirits.

Michael Charest, Kent Steen, and David Kazebee have been partners in the now moribund value driven technology company, AG Bill, which we hoped would contribute in a modest way to the improvement of medical care. Even when my writing distracted me from AG Bill activities, they were patient and supportive. One of them is also funny.

Most of all I especially acknowledge my parents, Belle and Sam (may they rest in peace), my mother-in-law Shirley Shils, my wife Ronnie and my son Eli, all of whom supported me and put up with my eccentricities. I love you all.

Carl S. Burak
July 4, 2006